KILLICK STONES

KILLICK STONES
A Collection of Maine Island Writing

Edited by
George Putz and Island Journal *Staff*

■

Illustrations by Bryan Wiggins

Island Institute
Rockland, Maine

The Island Institute gratefully acknowledges the support of the Charles Englehard Foundation in contributing toward production costs of Killick Stones.

© 1987 by Island Institute

Typography by High Resolution, Camden, Maine
Printed and bound by Western Maine Graphics, Inc., Norway, Maine
Cover and book design by Amy Fischer

Published by Island Institute
P.O. Box 429
Rockland, Maine 04841

Contents

Introduction

M *aine islands abound in writers.* As a group, writers tend to be
self-possessed — so are islands. Writers need peace and quiet
—islands offer this. Writers are often eccentric — so are islanders,
who can appreciate their own kind. Writers need vision and freedom
of expression — island air is clear, and islanders exercise great irony
to avoid mincing words. Good writers need a sense of humor (if they
are to save their prose or verse!) — when they're not driving you
nuts, islands make you laugh, amazed.

Too, islanders read. All the storm and fog that appears in island
literature is not a sentimental device created to move readers. It's just
there, and often. Most islanders are exceptionally literate because it
is distracting and comforting to read under environmental duress.
Island libraries are good ones, and regularly patronized. Writers,
reading, and islands go well together.

This first collection of island fiction comes to us at a peculiar time.
There are as many writers around as there ever have been; probably
more. And there is such an enormous amount of discretionary money
about. Island land values increase exponentially every year. . . . Yet,
there has been a dearth of island fictional writing, lasting now for

almost two decades. To some degree the publishing business is at fault. Mergers favoring bottom-line business management and systems are partly to blame, but so is the Maine literary community. There is in our land an escape from sentiment and an embrace of *prose-verité*, as it were — a need by the privileged to bathe in the deprivations they were somehow denied. All the "best" Maine literature in recent times has been about rural poor people, their psycho- and social pathologies. These books have been wonderfully written. As in so many so-called "movements," the appreciative, largely critical and academic audience has tended to confuse form with content, and so now it has become not just *de rigueur* and hip to celebrate cultural deprivations without sentiment, but mandatory.

From an island perspective, this is nonsense. All resident native islanders have significant poverty and deprivation in their personal and family histories and are not inclined to use their natal literacy in its celebration — except to appreciate good writing. Our instincts are framed by sentiment, and since no aware person can step ashore on an island and not be moved by its being, all islands are inherently sentimental places. Most island writing is sentimental to some degree. To deem it therefore not good writing is stupid.

We call this our *first* volume of island fiction to looming good purpose. The island grapevine, and a single plain announcement in the newsletter of the Maine Writers and Publishers Alliance brought in over 40 manuscripts, from which we have chosen these nine stories and two pieces of literary criticism. Many others were worthy, so, clearly, succeeding volumes of island fiction will be forthcoming. If you are a writer, or you know writers, be encouraged to send material our way. This first book is not a large one, partly out of shyness and trepidation, but also to give a generation one last chance to brag about the "old days" when books were a mere six bucks. If nothing else, show this to your grandchildren! But, know too that this volume could have been larger, and more expensive. With your good readership and encouragement, there will be subsequent books of new fiction to keep the islands of Maine in the lights of New England literature where they have always deserved to be.

George Putz
Island Institute
Rockland, Maine

Ruth Moore
Tongue of Granite, Tongue of Salt

Gary Lawless

There is a quotation from a patriarch of Zen Buddhism: "To seek one's own true nature is a way to lead you to your long-lost home."

I speak of the work of the Maine novelist Ruth Moore. I do not speak as a critic, but as a writer responding to the work of another writer. I speak as a native, hearing the language of home. Reading Ruth Moore's work is, for me, a way of leading myself to a long-lost home.

She begins her first novel, *The Weir*, by saying, "That was the place you were homesick for, even when you were there." Moore's work creates (or re-creates) a community, a community of many lives, many rhythms and cycles, breath and life. Her work is a landscape, a geography. Her work is the voice of water against rock, a littoral voice. Tongues of granite, tongues of salt. Voices heard on the wind. I have come to believe that it is actually the land itself, the community of things speaking through Ruth Moore. Her writing gives voice to place, a quite specific place.

So let's begin with a quote from the poet William Stafford:

> All events and experiences are local, somewhere. And all human en-
> hancements of events and experiences . . . all the arts . . . are regional in
> the sense that they derive from immediate relation to felt life.
>   It is this immediacy that distinguishes art. And paradoxically the
> more local the feeling in art, the more all people can share it, for that
> vivid encounter with the stuff of the world is our common ground.
>   Artists, knowing this mutual enrichment that extends everywhere,
> can act, and praise, and criticize, as insiders — the means of art is the life
> of all people. And that life grows and improves by being shared. Hence,
> it is good to welcome any region you live in or come to think of, for that
> is where life happens to be, right where you are.

Stafford says that it is "good to welcome any region you live in." It is
really important to emphasize the word "in," — to live "in" the
region rather than on top of it, to be a part of the region's natural
rhythms and cycles, the voices of place, and to welcome the place
into your life, your work. To derive writing from the "immediate
relation to felt life." Stafford feels that this encounter is our common
ground. This is the common ground on which the reader meets Ruth
Moore. She is giving voice to a very particular place. It is identifiable,
locatable, imaginable. It feels real. The *New York Times* has said of
her work, "It is doubtful if any American writer has ever done a better
job of communicating a people, their talk, their thoughts, their
geography, and their way of life."

Ruth Moore's books are rich with information, specific information given in a very precise, correct language, preserving a way of life
in a particular community now lost to us. The place has changed, the
people have changed, yet we can look to her books for accurate
depictions of the lives lived within this place.

I want here to quote from an essay on Ruth Moore written by
Donald F. Mortland and published in the *Colby Library Quarterly*
(Vol. XV #1, March 1979):

> Piles of books have been written about the Maine coast and its people,
> some of which are sentimental slush, some simply wrong . . . There are
> several ruinous rocks to be skirted in writing about the Maine coast.
> One is the danger of being sentimental. Another is the tendency to be
> folksy. A third is the danger of falling into ruts made by previous writers
> that lead into folksy stories about quaint people with hearts of gold who

speak a peculiar dialect, mourn about the past, and spend their lives dealing with trivia over which the author makes them triumphant in some miniscule way. Ruth Moore avoids all of these.

Each place has its own rhythms and cycles, its own language. There are ways of living in a place that are in harmony with these rhythms, and there are ways of living in a place that are destructive to these rhythms. We can live in place, mindful of these rhythms, attempting to attune ourselves with them, or we can bring other ways of living, other ways of seeing and doing, from elsewhere and destroy the local, natural rhythms, changing the place forever.

As writers we can draw deeply on the spirit of place, tuning in to the cycles, plant and animal, air and water, and seeing how these cycles move in the depths of our own imaginations. In Ruth Moore's work we draw on five generations of living in place, a long-term devotion and attention to place, and a deep relationship between lives led, language and imagination. Action here is understood in relation to place, and the structure of the story involves the structures of life around it. A long-term residence in a specific place brings to the writer a deeper understanding of action in terms of consequence, the ripples, pools, and long-term effects that are usually not obvious.

A place is a form and has its own influences on the literary form that is created within it. If we do things which are not in harmony with the place, we destroy the place or exile ourselves from it. We become lost because we cannot see where we are. We are uprooted, the strength of our vision is gone, and the reader follows our lead. We then speak as outsiders, and however well-intentioned, we do damage to the place with our images, our ideas and our representations.

I feel this is happening here in Maine, that the language and literature are becoming "gentrified " and actually removed from the "Real Maine" while supposedly portraying it. One critic has said that "because of the cliché that 'dirty' facts are real, and imaginative perceptions and truths are 'unreal,' the best fiction talents of our time are reporting on less than half of our life — the lower half."

Ruth Moore has written that she has tried "to write, as truthfully and accurately as I could, about small communities and the life in them which I have known well." She told the *Bangor Daily News*, "My object is to interpret this region realistically. After all, I grew up in it."

She was recently quoted as enjoying Carolyn Chute and Sanford Phippen because "both of them are telling the truth about a segment of Maine life — a segment that isn't in accord with the fairyland view of Maine put out by the Maine Publicity Bureau."

The *New York Times* noted her "authentic feeling for place, for the true and ordinary values of every day, the meaningfulness of independence, of work, of honesty and kindness." Another reviewer called this her "beautiful explicitness of time and place and individuals."

I feel that there is a sense of healing in Ruth Moore's fiction, a sense of balancing, the loss of balance and balance restored. Characters, emotions, community and the natural world are pictured in various states of balance and imbalance. Long before the "New Maine Fiction" we find the subjects of abuse, alcoholism, racism, sexism, family violence, and murder portrayed, but with a wonderful sense of balance, of being within a larger community. We are not rolled in the mud, nor flown to heights of romanticism. All endings are not happy, but we are given full characters, rich characters — people we feel we have known, and communities we could call home.

In her novel *The Fire Balloon*, Moore writes that her character, Roger, "came to feel an almost mystic relationship with the region of lakes and forests, the ocean shorelines and the windy islands off the coast, set with their green and secret trees. He was aware at times of a deep inner homesickness for a place of mind which he had known as a young man trying to write poems, a place still and solitary where he had been able to listen and set down some part of what he heard." This is what I think Moore has done with her work, to listen and set down some part of what she has heard.

* * * * *

Ruth Moore was born on July 21, 1903, on Gotts Island (or Great Gott Island). Gotts Island had a steady population from the 1780s to the late 1920s. There are reports of French settlers there around 1680. Champlain called it Petit Plaisants. In 1789 the island was purchased by Daniel Gott and its name changed.

Moore's family lived on the island for five generations. Her father Philip Moore was the island's postmaster, in addition to running a small store and a herring weir. The Moores also boarded the school-teacher. Ruth graduated from Ellsworth High School and went on to graduate from New York State College for Teachers in Albany in

1925. For the next 20 years she spent most of her time away from Maine, working as a teacher, as a secretary in both New York and California, and as an associate editor of *The Reader's Digest.* A long poem, "The Voyage," was published in the *Saturday Review of Literature* in May of 1929. Several of her short stories appeared in *The New Yorker* and *Harpers Bazaar.* She was 40 when her first novel went to a publisher. The first five had been set aside, but the sixth went out. She was living in San Francisco at the time "doing jobs I disliked. Further, the climate there simply didn't agree with me." Her first novel, *The Weir,* was published by William Morrow and Company in 1943.

When Ruth Moore was growing up, and while she was away, her home on Gotts Island was going through a transition. Most families were fishing and lobstering families, with small gardens and perhaps a cow. The attraction of the mainland was having a strong effect on the community. People were going there to sell fish and lobsters, to buy supplies, to go to school, and to have many of the conveniences which town life provided.

From the 1890s the summer visitors gradually discovered the island. The Moores were among the first to take in boarders. Summer homes were built, land changed hands, and the island economy changed. Moore writes about the process in *Candlemas Bay:*

> Jen and her kind were everywhere. To them the wonderful heritage of a house and land meant nothing but how they could use it to make money out of the summer people. Sell the land for summer cottages. Fill up the house with boarders for a season or so, remodel it into a hotel. Then would come a bad year when the summer trade didn't show up, and the hotel would fail. There it would stand, windows broken out, doors banging in the wind, paint scaling off, an eyesore to the countryside. No good to anyone. Like the Griswold house. . . .
>
> And where were the Griswolds now? Their land was sold, the money spent. The womenfolks of the younger generation were working in the sardine factories, trying to keep their families' heads above water; or they were cooks and maids in the summer cottages. Their menfolks were caretakers or gardeners or deckhands on somebody's yacht. In the wintertime, none of them had any work. They lived on credit from the grocery stores, and during the Depression they'd had to take food from the government.

In 1927 the house and barn of Clarence Harding burned. Also in 1927 Washington decided to discontinue the post office on Gotts

Island. These two events mark a finality in the history of the island, and almost all of the permanent residents had left by the end of the year, including the Moores.

The Weir chronicles this transitional period from the points of view of several characters, including Hardy, based on her father. Hardy is the last to fish with a weir but is torn by his longing for something else, perhaps to open a store on the mainland. He longs for the peace of mind and security which had been on the island but was no longer there. It was the same island, changed only by cleared fields and snug houses, which in the 1700s had meant home and harbor, an island wrapped around by water, set off from the world by a curtain of peaceful sound, which was the sound of water hanging in the air. Existence had been sweetened and protected here, but now people groped after that safety, feeling it lost. If it were not here, then it must be somewhere else — Hardy feels the island, gone to seed.

And yet once they have left the island, the land stays in their minds and hearts:

> Days in the fall, when the leaves were yellow and the sky that color it gets, and the air blew down over the town, cool and crisp and all but snapping, he felt like taking off for some place back of beyond, at a dead run — run and run until he got back that lean, limber feeling he'd had all his life, up to now. All at once, the island which he'd been so crazy to leave, had seemed like heaven to him.
>
> He'd wake up nights, thinking about it; sometimes the color of the water behind the breakwater, that deep green when it lay in the shadow, or the sound the ducks made as they scaled down into the pond in the swamp.

To digress for a moment, I have found that there is a special place in these novels for the swamp. In *Spoonhandle* Moore's character Mag has returned to the island and bought the swamp:

> (She) remembered the swamp of old. It was a secret and private place where nobody went. All her life she had thought of it, off and on . . . There in the back of her mind would be lying, quiet and cool, a picture of the old Stilwell swamp, its ferns and its moss and its crooked tree roots, its black pools edged with green, the alders thick as a man's leg growing between the aisles of the spruces. She remembered the Salt Pond Water, emptying and filling twice a day, and the lookout from the footbridge, and the soft sound of the ebb and flood under it. Some days,

she told herself, thinking about such things was about all that kept her
a-goin.

And from *Speak To The Winds*:

The swamp flowered all summer, no matter how dry the season. Above
it, the granite crisped its lichens in the sun, baked as fiercely dry as if the
heat had struck outward from its furnace fires within. But the growth
around the pool stayed brilliant electric green. Alders grew thick as a
man's thigh, and some of the old swamp birches were three feet
through at the base. Tall trees and the hill kept away the wind, so that
the air hung hot and still, full of rich jungle smells of mud and moss and
lush, sunny leaves. Squirrels lived in the swamp, and deer and mink and
beaver and muskrat. Hermit thrushes sang there all spring long. The
trees were full of wing-flash and flutter and the four or five clear notes,
repeated a thousand times, of the white-throated sparrow. Ducks gathered in the pond; at fall dusk it might be brimful of them, floating side by
side. To these inhabitants, at any time of the year, the swamp offered
shelter, either of shade or snow.

Moore's second novel, *Spoonhandle*, brought her home. Shortly
after its publication in 1946, interest was shown in turning it into a
play. Twentieth Century Fox offered more money and it instead
became the movie *Deep Water*, filmed on the Maine coast with Dana
Andrews, Jean Peters, Dean Stockwell, and Ed Begley. The author
feels that the movie "butchered" her book. She had been under
contract to write the scenario but found that she hadn't developed
the technique and passed the job along. The movie did allow her
financially to return to Maine with the freedom to write.

In 1947 she returned to Maine and spent the summer on Gotts
Island. She and Eleanor May (who has also published novels based in
the same region) built their own home and workshop in McKinley,
on Mt. Desert just across from the island.

One of the central characters in *Spoonhandle* is Anne Freeman, a
young woman who is returning to the island after spending some
time in New York and publishing her first book. She has come to
work on a second book.

As in *The Weir*, we see an island community in transition, to which
Anne returns from the city:

I had a lot of fine foolish rapture about living simply and doing good simple hard work. . . . I'm scared of this part of the country. It's bleak and unyielding. Here people start to go down for the third time and every-body knows it, but nobody does anything. In the city you've made a place for yourself, you know your way around, you can go out and get a job. . . .

Yet she is looking for a chance to think without being driven. She wonders why she has returned to a place she fought to escape from — and if her work fails, where will she go, what will she do?

This place here, this countryside, was what she loved and wanted fiercely to be a part of, yet the way she was now, divided, it hadn't anything to offer her.

I guess I'd like to belong somewhere, she told herself forlornly, but I'd have to guess again to know for sure where. . . .

During the busy years, the wild and solitary beauty of the eastern shore had almost gone out of her mind — at least, it was still wild and solitary if she kept to the stretches of shore line that remained where summer cottages weren't under construction.

Wandering along the shore, she could feel no reality in the fact that everything was sold now, the acres which for so many generations had belonged to the Freeman family. The place was the same — except for the growth of the spruces and a few alder thickets which had sprung up here and there, she couldn't see any change. She told herself that she hadn't any right to feel at home here, but it didn't do any good. The sense of at-homeness, of belonging, almost a sense of possession, stayed automatically in the back of her mind. Even while she walked along saying to herself, In a few months there'll be a fat, ten- or fifteen-room house right here, probably showing a Georgian influence, and a tiled swimming pool dug into Apple Cove Beach — could be, with steam-pipes to heat the salt water, that was the kind of thing they did — even while her reason said this to her, the land, something else said, was the Freeman land and always would be.

It seemed absurd; but there it was — not actually regret that the land was sold, but more a habit of thinking, as if a feeling for land might be hereditary, transmitted as naturally as the color of eyes and hair, through chromosomes. She hadn't realized, before, that she'd feel like that. She would have thought she'd been away from the eastern shore too long. But, apparently, it was something you didn't get over. . . .

Everything is so dull and drab. But don't you know its full of marvels. . . .

It's natural, I guess, to want to see other places than the one you know. But people are the same anywhere, wonderful, tragic, and places. . . . They had to find out for themselves. No one could tell them.

It is Anne's need to write that brings her home, and that gives her more insight into the people around her:

> She'd learned to write, concentrating on the impact, the effect of human beings on one another, for that, in essence, was what you tried to do. She'd begun to understand a little better the insecurities, the frustrations that made a man like her father act like he did. She learned to take the trouble to find out and understand the inner stresses and strains that made people need to interfere with other people, most often the ones they knew best and loved.

Out of this looking at the effect of human beings on one another Moore creates a complex community of characters. Anne's place within the community, as a writer and a woman, is tentative. People know that she has written a book, and seem pleased and proud, but few have actually read the book. In her short story, "The Soldier Shows His Medal," Moore explains:

> The year I myself was 20, I published a poem in a little magazine, dead now these many years, both poem and magazine forgotten. It wasn't much . . . but I remember how I wanted people to know. They never did, for whenever it was on my lips to tell, I kept hearing the neighbors: "Guess she thinks she's something, bragging about her writing being printed, somewheres to the west'ard."

This leads us to another major theme in Ruth Moore's work — the roles of women within the community. In the first two novels we meet women who have gone away from the island and have returned with a wider view of themselves and the world.

Anne Freeman in *Spoonhandle* returns only to be met at the dock by insulting behavior from the local store owner:

> The neat way in which with three words he had turned her into a silly interfering female had made her angry, but something else too. It had been a long time since she had encountered indifferent disregard of herself as a thinking human being — so long that she had almost forgotten how it felt.

She'd expected it. That was the way men here were to their women-folk; you couldn't count on any change. She'd had it and fought it, all through her childhood and youth. What it had done was to make her try hard, discipline herself, train her mind into a tool that could give her back some self-respect. . . .

(Actions such as his made you) wonder if there weren't some common ground on which human beings could meet without trying to wrench each other out of shape. If you took the trouble, couldn't you find out and understand the inner stresses and strains that made people need to interfere with other people?

The books in high school had never given her an idea of any work she could do, nor of how she could best go about doing it if she knew what it was. What they had given her was a restless craving energy, a determination not to let the worth she had be wasted. She didn't suppose she wanted everything in the world — only to live her life so that it made sense.

But when Anne returns to the island, there is a fisherman who wants to marry her. She questions what would happen to her if she were to marry him, as she looks around at the other women in the community:

She knew well enough what it would mean if she got married and stayed here at the harbor. The tired, discouraged women and girls whom she saw every day were evidence enough. They kept house for the menfolk and children at night, and worked in the sardine factory in the daytime. The day's work most of them put in was too much for any woman to stand, and they showed it in the way they looked and the way they dragged around.

Not that she minded hard work — she'd certainly done enough of it, but to struggle along like that, to know your menfolk expected it of you, would take the heart out of any woman.

She considers marrying the man, and wonders what would become of her own individuality:

Would he make a companion of her, let her have a part in the important things of his life — she didn't think that he would. He'd look on her as something he possessed, to make love to, to keep his house and make him comfortable, something less than a person who had the same kind of brains and feelings he did. The men around here all felt that way about women.

Like Anne Freeman, many of the characters in Ruth Moore's community are trying to live a decent, quiet life. She says in *The Weir* that "most people would be OK, if other people would let them alone." In several novels central characters are children, many of them with bad childhood experiences — orphans, "state" children, runaways, and children of alcoholics. In *Candlemas Bay* she says, "You were all so beautiful when you began, before the world and your lives flowed up over you like a sea." The author has a great depth of sympathy for them. In *Sea Flower* she talks about not offending the little ones:

> That word offend. . . . It meant to harm them inside in a way they never got over. How many people did you see, well, not all, but an awful lot of them, grown up, man-grown out of offended little ones, who might have been twice-three times what they were, if it hadn't been for the harm? They got it early and they kept it going, passed it along the way they passed the color of their hair and their eyes, so it never died out, but got to be as much a part of the human race as legs and fingers. Look at the way they mistreated everything that couldn't fight back, give a wound. Animals. Birds. Look, for Godsakes, at the way they mistreated trees. Offend — probably the real work on earth of the devil. . . .
> Animals had no recourse against human beings: in the end, animals always lost. It did seem that mankind, so marvelous in many ways, and Nature's finest achievement through millions of centuries of trial and error, should know what itself was, without having to prove supremacy, again and again, with blood and terror, over organisms weaker and less fortunate.

The speaker goes on to say, "I am a solitary man for that reason. I haven't ever been able to stand it." And later he says that "what a man is used to is a cup of coffee and his own shoestrings and tomorrow, and standing on the beach looking at the water and saying God, ain't that pretty."

In each of her books there are one or two characters who choose to live alone, apart, to separate themselves from the push and pull life of the community, "not because they are different from anyone else (and if you live apart, people begin to think that you are) but because they like to." Her character Willie, in *Spoonhandle*, is not a violent man but one who can't stand the "pull and haul between people" and chooses to come away by himself. It is this "pull and haul," this "effect of human beings on one another" which lies at the core of each Moore novel.

Another character, in *A Fair Wind Home*, considers the life apart:

It might be lonesome for awhile. But a picture floated before his mind of small, solitary beaches, dreaming in the sun, silent woods, sun-spangled stretches of water. No people with their complications to burst in tangling up your life and your privacy, pressing their concerns, their wishes, their problems on you, until your own life seemed to dwindle, until you had no life at all you could call your own.

For a man to live a simple, honest life, not breaking his neck to get money, not kicking his neighbors in the face for it — he admired that way of living. . . .

Their love of the countryside went back and back. It was hereditary, almost, like something in the genes, understandable since their people had wrestled a hard living for generations out of this rock. But if you knew so much, if you knew how to cope, to handle, to deal with, why should this not make you the more confident, why should you not the better enjoy?

Many of her plots revolve around small misunderstandings or quarrels which start innocently enough but soon have whole families and groups of islanders lined up against each other. Consider these excerpts:

Sometimes I think it is not the forces of nature we have so much to fear, but the ill-will over little things that breaks out of even good Christian men.

Not the place; there was nothing in places for a man to fear. The natural disasters — two storms meeting overhead and bashing it out together, lightning striking, the sea rolling up to drown — were land and sea and sky and weather, minding their own business. They were what a man coped with the best he could, but not afraid so much as watchful. Death in its own good time, but in between, breakfast and birds' nests, the birds on the trees, apples and sunsets, grass with dew on it, a winter overcoat, a man's wife and his children, spring coming and full-turned leaves, a hot buttered rum on a cold night, and clean spruce chips and clam chowder and snow. Not the place or the dark, or the nightmare of the bears' woods; but the malice, the ill-will, the rancor, running like pus out of the minds of men. . . .

She knew what an island row meant. They started over trifles and snowballed on trifles until whole families took sides, down to the children, and for months, years sometimes, people didn't speak or have anything to do with each other.

People don't want to hear about using each other decent. They'd a damn sight rather sit around and shake over the idea of a puddle of hell fire waiting for them, or for the world to come to an end. It's more fun. Besides, to be decent means a certain amount of give and take. Most people would rather see everything smashed up than give one goddamn inch.

No one would have to set his mind on finding a grudge or two to smolder over, the island being what it was, people living for years in each other's placket holes.

Town rows. Sometimes they got better, sometimes worse. The thing grew like a tumor. And when a row really got rolling and hate and violence took over, you couldn't stop it; it had to run its course. Usually, when it was over, you found more damage had been done than anybody could afford. . . .

People think, a good fight will help us get through the winter. That was just the trouble. Too many people, in the beginning, thought they might enjoy a fight, not figuring ahead to when it might end. . . .

Stick your nose in somebody's business, get just about what you asked for. A fight was like a teeter-board; you hurt somebody and you went up, they hurt you back and you went down. It got going faster and faster; winding up tighter and tighter, until what you saw everywhere was ill-will; and you no longer wished for things to be righted, but for yourself to be appeased, to be in the acknowledged right of it . . . for the world to come on bended knee. . . .

Good juicy venom of this kind was meat and drink to Flo. "You know full and well," she told her friends, "I speak no evil of anybody, but the only liveable, nameable thing in my mind always and forever is the good of this town. *But.* . . . "

It was a decent town. . . . He didn't have many illusions about his neighbors. Some might think they weren't so tough and competent as the old-timers who had built the town, but he was a long ways from believing that. You had to take into consideration what worry and being in debt and scraping along on the skin of your teeth year in and year out would do to a man; three-quarters of the time, no work and no prospects, sandpapering away at him till he wore thin; until, if he didn't say to hell with it, he acted as if he might, any time, and the summer people, seeing how he was, wagged heads as if at a funeral, saying it was too bad, a fine old solid section of the country was petering out.

But let some project come up where a man felt he was useful and needed, or an emergency. . . . You would see the old toughness, the old competence, the old skills come out overnight, and none of them rickety, either, from lack of use. . . .

One town, this size, it doesn't amount to much; but the world, after all, is only a mess of towns, some big, some small. The history of the world's nothing but town records, records of one kind or another, records of government. And government, when you boil it down, is decent people getting together and making decent laws for themselves to live decently by. If you have it, you've got the best there is so far; if you don't have it, you've got nothing — a mess of thieves and pirates.

To add to the quarrels, to the movement away from the islands to the mainland, the transition of the community, we have the advent of the "Summer People." The summer people found Gotts Island late in the 1800s as they worked their way along the Maine coast. Ruth Moore's family was one of the first on the island to take in boarders.

The summer people signal a major shift. While changing the economy of the community, they also change the way the local people view themselves, their land and their community:

They say there's quite a lot of summer people wants to buy places on this island. Be a wonderful thing for the town; if only they did start to come here more, wouldn't it?

Would be if you like summer people.

Well, of course nobody likes them. They have t'be waited on hand and foot, and frigged with, and they act like they was God Almighty. But they do bring a lot of money and work to a town. . . .

The summer people acted like royalty, with royalty's gracious, condescending manners, and the local people took it for granted. "Why Colonel Swansley told me," she was saying with pride, "that I was the only housekeeper he ever had whom he considered worthy to mingle with his guests." Bellport, from a village of independent fishermen and farmers, their own men who took nothing from anybody, had become a townful of domestic servants.

One of the summer people in Moore's work thinks to himself:

What he wanted now, more than anything, was to be the center of some small world, where simple, kindly people looked up to him — not because of money or favors they could expect, but sincerely. Bellport was too full of his own kind, of too many who wished to be looked up to, some of them able to command more respect than he. The little place on the island was to be a kind of manor house, with himself in it, through the mellow summers of his declining years, dispensing jobs and advice.

Another summer visitor speaks:

I quarrel with Mr. Clawson about coming to these dead little towns but you know it's such a relief to me to be away from it all, where there isn't one thing to attract my attention and no so-called interests — except, of course, the natives. I'm always interested in them. You see, in a small way, I'm a sociologist. I hope someday to have enough material for a book on rural customs and the economic life of these people. . . .

We've been in many of these coast towns, Mr. Clawson and I. I find their economic situation most interesting. . . . Here you have some of the oldest towns in the country falling into decay because, with changing conditions, there's not enough work to support their people. I understand this entire region was once farming and fishing communities. Now, of course, it's largely summer-resident property.

The solution would be so simple, if they only had a little gumption. . . . Your local people have no place here any longer. If there are no jobs, they should pick up themselves and their families and go elsewhere, where they can find work. But will they? No.

They cling like limpets to their old way of life, the life their fathers set up here and which is now gone. They squabble like crows over the few paying jobs there are. And each year we come back, we see them still poorer, still nearer the — er — ragged edge than ever. They have only themselves to blame.

We're hospitable. We like to keep enough cooks and maids and chauffers around so that our summer visitors can be comfortable. A grocer, too. And one plumber and one electrician, so that lights and water in the cottages can be turned off in the fall and on in the spring.

Don't you think, Miss Ellis," she asked, fixing Candace with a narrowed, sociological eye, "that inbreeding in these coastal towns is responsible for so many feeble-minded children?"

But let the subject come up at any time and the thought was automatic — someone would be sure to express it too — the summer people were helpless, they didn't know how to cook or wash or clean or any of those things that really capable people knew how to do — like anything said over and over often enough, people would believe it, no matter how much proof to the contrary stared them in the face. Like still thinking of Miss Roxina as summer people, an outsider. You did and she was, and would be, if she stayed forever.

To Elbridge's way of thinking, if anybody lived in a place as an outsider, and looked, talked and acted different from everyone else, it was bound to have an effect. With anyone like that, ordinary things could be twisted around, quite easily, to look peculiar. Anybody who looked different, was different, was fair game.

In several of the novels we find these characters, outsiders who have chosen for various reasons to stay in the community. There is a Jewish schoolteacher, a Portuguese family, and rumors of "Nigger/ Wop/Indian" blood. At one point in *Speak To The Winds* one of the most spiteful characters forms a "Society of American Christians — No Foreigners or Niggers need apply."

But in the end, say from 1927 on Gotts Island, and in the finality of Ruth Moore's novels, it is the summer people who stay. The locals leave or their community, their culture, gradually disappears.

Everybody here has been twizzling like a windmill, for years, hoping he can sell his land to the summer people. You know that. This is the loveliest place on God's Green Earth, and no better anywhere for folks to live, if they want to try to live and make something of it. Why, people from away come and pay thousands of dollars, just so they can stay three months out of the year. But it's like anything else in the world — if you've got something that's worth something and you don't value it or take care of it, someone'll take it away from you, legally or otherwise. . . .

Think what you would about the offshore islands, love them as you must, they were still an enigma, a mystery. There they were, peaceful and lovely, the black trees with moonlight on them — places for a man to find his soul when he had lost it. But pitiless, silent, saying nothing back to warm flesh and blood. Sufficient to themselves, take them or leave them. People came, built houses; lived there, died; went away. . . .

Places for a man to find his soul, when he had lost it. What remains is the islander's sense of a place that had been, a slow moving memory of a place, changed forever, lost forever. A place "lovely as some place you might have made up in a daydream. Green, sleepy islands; little wooded coves, trees down to the water's edge; high granite bluffs; black bull-backed ledges where the surf washed over; water stretching away forever, blue, whitecapped, shining in the sun.

"That was the place that you were homesick for, even when you were there."

Gary Lawless is co-owner of Gulf of Maine Bookstore in Brunswick and publisher of Blackberry Books, which has recently reprinted three novels by Ruth Moore (*The Weir, Spoonhandle*, and *Speak To The Winds*). He lives at Chimney Farm, Nobleboro, Maine.

Island Girl

Catharine S. Baker

T his island hasn't got room for us any more. I saw it coming, and now it's here. They own the view, and the fact that we and our generations were here first is no more account than seagulls screaming. I'm not talking about the christly ferry lines, either. My family has always had boats and gone off the island when we wanted to. But now we can't go on the island. It don't belong to us no more. I'd like to burn those castles down, and their signs and fences. They will shame you in front of any passing dog, like you was one.

Take the other day — I was home by four because I skipped lunch, and I says to my daughter, "Tammy, let's take a hike up to the graveyard. I got this plastic arrangement for Gram's grave. It's nice out. Do you good."

"Naah. Karen said she'd call me. We might go up to the store."

I counted the petals on one of the yellow roses with the edge of my fingernail. I thought of several things I might say, any of which would have been an improvement on what I felt like saying. I rejected "She said that two days ago and you still ain't seen her." Also "Get off your fat butt before you need a block and tackle." I tried, "Hon, you look

21

pale. There's a good breeze up there. When you're expecting, you have to take care of yourself." It sounded like something someone else would say, but oddly enough it worked. Probably just the sort of thing mothers say in those afternoon shows. She's gotten into those.

So we went, waddle waddle. She's wearing her brother Fred's old woods jacket and I've got my parka I used to go get fir tips in. It's clear, bright and lonely. All the alder leaves have curled. They don't turn colors, just roll up brown like someone had started in making cigars and given it up as unprofitable. The smell of the fields is, well, bitter somehow. I know how a hayfield should smell, we made pretty fair hay when I was a kid, but these little meadows down here have all gone to rank weeds, redtop, asters, goldenrod, and dogbane. All you can say is it smells like fall.

The little birds that are in the fields in summer have gone. Someone forgot to tell the old hawk, though. Sharpshins, sharp eyes, aglitter on the dead spruce at the end of our road. Tammy got spooked at him and threw a rock.

"Someone tell you hawks eat people? That's vultures, and they have to be dead. The people, I mean."

"I know, I know. He was giving me the evil eye. I do not need the evil eye on me. I need good luck charms," and she started singing this rock-and-roll song about the evil eye lady who has charms to sell. I've heard it.

"Well, for good luck you can't beat a double-ring rock. We should stop down to the beach. It's not far." God, it's like a million miles, back to when she and Fred would be down there hunting magic rocks. They would always manage to fight over one, many as there are on that stone beach. We made our way through the blackberry canes and alder trash. The path used to be a kid highway. Now the summer people have it all to themselves, with their Dobermans and their Private Property No Trespassing signs every six inches. They're gone now, though. All you'll meet is their donkey-man, guard dog Mallory, checking it out, and that's pretty rarely.

So we went down onto the beach, to the edge of the shingle, and hunted up a good rock. I love the feel of a beach pebble. When I first went over to work at the Mart, I always kept one in my apron pocket to rub and feel when I was getting lectured to by the French poodle there, Mrs. Collins of Customer Relations. It helped a good deal. I thought maybe Tammy could use one. She used to be the biggest collector of trash you ever saw. Doing her wash was life endangering, with the stuff in the pockets. You'd put your hand in and wish you hadn't. She was much worse that way than either of the boys.

She was poking and stooping, with grunts, when I heard a halloo. I stopped in my tracks, I didn't like the sound. I looked all around me to see where it had come from. Damned if someone wasn't yelling and waving from the porch of one of those new summer places that isn't a cottage but built where one was. Cars were in the drive. They hadn't gone home. They were staying down, might be living there if you can call that living — all so neat, no wash out, just walls of glass. They didn't want us in the view out their windows, I could tell. I decided to ignore the whole thing.

"Tammy, let's go up the beach a bit."

"Ma, who is that yelling? I didn't know anybody was still down here. Whoever it is, he's mad." She was right about that.

"Don't pay them any mind. We aren't hurting the beach any, walking on it." But she was nervous now, she gets self-conscious around strangers. You'd think it was the old days when a girl that was pregnant was never seen outdoors. I didn't want to shame her. So I kept walking, eyes sharp for a lucky stone, and she came along, muttering to herself.

But we wasn't fast enough. Damned if this old carcase doesn't come right down on us, down his seawall or whatever, even though we were well on our way and out of his.

"You people are on private property, are you aware of that?"

I wasn't going to answer someone who used that tone with me. I knew where I was, knew a hell of a lot more about it than he did. He thinks his beach is cast in bronze; I know how much it's moved and will move in the next storm. I kept going.

"This isn't a public right-of-way, if it ever was. This land is posted and belongs to the Association."

This land comes and goes of its own free will, you rich bastard.

"If you people don't depart immediately the way you came, I will have to document this intrusion for my lawyer." I spun around then. It wasn't enough that he was running us off and Tammy was starting to cry because she was humiliated by it, but he was going to take pictures. I swear, there he was with a camera. I couldn't stand there for that.

I yelled at him, "You think because you have money up your ass that you own this. Well you don't. My people dug clams here and had clam feeds and beached their boats and spread their nets and made weirs and walked on this beach before your kind ever heard of this island. This don't belong to you or anyone else but the tide. And I'll leave the way I please."

He started coming closer, he had his camera up to his face, I could hear him taking pictures of me shouting, and Tammy trying to hide her face because she wished she'd never been born. I know I shouldn't have done it, but he was trying to trap me, he kept moving closer with no eyes but his camera like a mask, he wasn't human. I know I shouldn't have but I had that lucky rock and I threw it and hit that camera. I am a good hand chucking rocks. It broke something, I can tell. He ran and screamed for help. We hustled off the other way.

I had left my arrangement for the grave up in the alders; and I meant to go fetch it and get on my way. Tammy wasn't having any more. She wanted to go home. "I ain't coming out for a week. Ma, they are going to send the sheriff after you."

"Perhaps they are. It's all on film. Nothing to hide any more. I guess I'll just go on. The flaming bastard! They want us all in the kennel, come out for dog duty when they whistle — nice dog, come clean up this mess. Well, I'm fed up to the eyelashes. Let him drag the whole shebang and shingle into the courts. They say every dog can have its day. I guess I'll have mine before we're done."

I was talking to myself by now. Tammy was doing her best to hustle back up the road to home. She had got an airing, all right. I imagine she thinks I arranged it all to make her feel like a freak, and she has enough troubles. I went on up to the graveyard on the Head. There really is a good breeze there. The old folks liked a view, too. They don't have no objection to sharing it, though.

I set there awhile on the stone wall, looking down the lane all grown up with weeds. They only mow for the hearse to come through, which is often enough the way the old island people are dying off. The young have gone to the mainland for work, and then when they want to come back to live they can't afford the land they left. Pretty soon the whole place will be like that little old graveyard — fenced off, with little markers for where the people used to be. I get real cheerful after a spell of sitting up there.

I started down, thinking what I could do for Tammy to make her feel like she had a right to be walking around inside her skin. It doesn't help to have a loudmouth mother, not when your personal preference would be invisibility. She's always been that way, too. It's not being pregnant with no engagement ring; that's just the latest in a long string of disasters styled with her in mind, the way she sees it. She'll probably get in high gear now about going ashore to live with her father's sister, where no one knows her. That's the whole problem, though. They aren't the least interested in having her. She won't fit in with their life style, they said. She's just an island girl, doesn't know how to mix with people she didn't grow up with.

I scooted on home, crosslots through the pasture. They're schooling in the channel, all right, them sharks. I told Tammy later, getting supper, the island isn't big enough, even with the tide out all the way. But I will have my day, all right. I will show my face. Just you wait and see.

Catharine Baker was born and raised in Damariscotta and Newcastle, farmed for four years in Edmunds Township, and began to write fiction a few years ago. She edits a newsletter and is putting together an historical cookbook for First Universalist Church, Rockland. She is married to Nicholas Snow, painter and part-time lobsterman. She lives in Spruce Head, Maine.

Moths

Patricia R. Crossman

O n a Sunday evening in early June, Sandy Dimmock saw a moth on the Formica back splash of the sink. It was a very small moth, not more than one-half inch across the folded wings. It formed a perfect beige triangle, faintly spotted with brown, against the citron green of the Formica.

Sandy studied it while she washed the dishes.

On the Maine island where she lived year-round, moths usually didn't appear until the very end of June.

After she had wiped the dishes, she lifted the motionless creature carefully on a thin piece of cardboard and put it outside.

Later, as she went up to open the bedroom window, she saw another one on the outside of her window screen.

"It might even have been the same one," she said to her husband, Peter, when she came down.

She sat on the footstool in front of the Franklin stove, cradling a mug of mint tea.

"Do you know, Peter," she said, "that's the first time I ever saw a moth that didn't fly into the light."

27

She tapped the mug thoughtfully, then looked up and laughed. Peter bent forward and kissed her quickly, and she looked up into his face, her heart swelling at the familiar smell of him, the smoky quality of his grey eyes, the unruly thick brows that shadowed them.

"I love you," she whispered ducking her head into his flannel shirt, to hide the sudden tears in her eyes.

She tried, without success, to steel herself against the tides of emotion that seemed to wash through her being as if in answer to some primal rhythm.

"Likewise," Peter said, his hand cradling her head, pressing it against his chest. "You are my prim and proper little tea-drinker with the warm hands and heart."

He bent her face up and looked into her eyes. "No one knows you like I do, Sandy Dimmock."

She thought no more about moths that night.

In the morning she looked out on a world of dazzling clarity. The spruces on the headland were razor-sharp against the sky. Beach roses spilled over her stone wall, reaching for the sea. The rocks glistened on the beach, drenched by waves of incredible blue that shattered into fragments of light, over and over.

Sandy took her coffee out onto the grassy terrace. For moments she stood surveying her world, solitude and beauty hedged about by acres of woodland, the only access a quiet road that meandered off into the trees behind the house.

The house itself was low, its driftwood-grey shingles and wide-spread ells cupping the terrace like an amphitheater. Sandy moved to the stone wall that marked the seaward edge of the terrace and looked back at the house.

"Do I care for it too much?" she wondered. "Maybe it's wrong to place such importance on a structure, a thing. But I do love it. We've been so happy here."

She closed her eyes and listened to the sounds that accompanied all her days. She felt whole, healthy, safe.

Not like that terrible time after her mother died, and she had the miscarriage, when she'd felt shattered, fragmented, a lot of broken, painful pieces that would never, never again constitute a whole.

But Peter had saved her; Peter who knew she must come to the house her parents had shared for twenty-seven summers. Peter who knew it could be winterized and made into a snug year-round house.

It was a house with nothing but happy memories. Not like the apartment where they'd lived, the small rooms full of all the accumu-lated pain of those four months; the nightly visits to her mother in the hospital, the panic when that figure in the shadowed room became a remote stranger, the guilt she felt when she couldn't face one more encounter.

She opened her eyes. "I won't think about that," she said briskly. "I'll get at Peter's typing, then straighten up his desk, and hang a wash."

She walked toward the house, her rising anxiety soothed by the recitation of familiar chores.

When she reached for the screen door, there was a small moth poised on the edge of the door frame.

It didn't move when she opened the door and went inside.

By ten o'clock, she had the washer going, Peter's latest research notes typed, and his giant oak desk in some kind of order.

Six years had taught her to throw away, file, or cover nothing unless she checked with Peter. At first, the perpetual clutter had distressed her, but eventually she found it comforting, the evidence of her husband's presence, the paraphernalia of his intellectual life, so constant and familiar.

Since his sabbatical had begun, he worked harder than ever. No more daily preparation of lessons, no more midnight marking of exams, no intrusion of distraught parents seeking answers to urgent questions; just disciplined routine hours of uninterrupted research and writing.

After ten years of teaching natural science at the most prestigious private school in Connecticut, he had arrranged to take his eighteen-month leave to coincide with the move to the island house. He was researching material for a tenth-grade level text and his enthusiasm for the venture hadn't palled in seven months of isolation.

Twice a week, he took the ferry to the mainland and spent the day in libraries and museums, conferences with colleagues and browsing through private collections.

Usually he found the hour-long trip home exhilarating, and came in ravenous.

During the winter, he had missed half a dozen trips when bad storms kept the rugged steel ferry in her berth at the harbor end of the island.

They had both regarded those days as bonus "Sundays" when they could forget work, storms, and the outside world and play Scrabble or double solitaire, stoke up the fire and grill hot dogs, nap if they chose, or make love by firelight while snow thickened on the windowsills.

Sandy had settled into a routine herself. It seemed to contribute to the healing process. She abandoned her interest in gourmet cooking.

"We're living in the middle of the ocean," Peter urged, "Let's make the most of it!"

So they ate haddock, clams and mussels, even New England boiled dinners, redolent of cabbage, with Sandy's crusty yeast breads or biscuits.

Most of the time, she was almost content.

She turned from the token neatness of the desk to Peter's drawing table. It was covered with pen and ink drawings, pencil sketches, one or two small completed water colors, all thumb-tacked or Scotch-taped to a particular spot.

Sandy bent over a pen drawing of a leaf, its veins exquisitely displayed. It lay on the paper like a living thing.

She felt the faint thrill that always accompanied her appreciation of Peter's brilliance.

In water color, an emerald-throated hummingbird danced ecstatically before a honeysuckle blossom. A stark birch tree stood lifeless among its green companions, its trunk girdled by some bark-eating animal.

Beside that sketch was a small painting of a tightly curved leaf, its underside an unpleasant green. On the edge of the picture there was a tiny tan moth.

"What is this?" Sandy said, aloud. "A plague?" She carried the paper to the side door and shook it. The moth fell into a bed of petunias and vanished.

She carefully placed the painting exactly where she'd found it, at the right-hand edge of the drawing board. As she taped it in place, she noticed an infinitesimal moth painted below the curled leaf, hardly more than a speck.

I must tell Peter how life-like his illustrations are, she thought. They even bring a living member of the species to check them out!

When Peter drove in, just after six o'clock, the back seat of their compact car was loaded with books and pamphlets.

"What's all this?" Sandy asked, leaning in his window for a kiss.

"Works on Lepidoptery. I'm at that point now in the text, and it's a fascinating field, endlessly complex. I've got to filter out all the extraneous stuff and put the nitty-gritty into no more than two chapters."

"All that? About Lepidoptera? I thought a moth was a moth!"

"A moth is an object of superstition in some cultures, a clothes-eating nuisance in all cultures, and a terrifying creature of the night in a few remote places where he grows to impressive size."

"Really." Sandy made a face. "Sounds wonderful, if you like your moths big and scary. I'm perfectly happy with the little fellows I see around here!"

She helped him carry the books into the house.

"Where are you going to put these?" she said, looking helplessly around his study. "Every square inch is covered!"

"Stack 'em on the floor."

"Pretty soon I won't be able to push a vacuum through here!"

"So? Seems like a perfect excuse to avoid housework. When I get the other rooms filled up, we'll camp on the beach and you can loaf all day."

"I love taking care of this house. *This* room you can fill. But leave the rest alone!"

"I think you have a nesting instinct," Peter said, reaching for her across the pile of books.

"You know I have," Sandy whispered, her face suddenly sober.

"I'm sorry, honey," he took her hand and put it against his face, "that wasn't a very thoughtful thing to say."

"But it's true, Peter. I want to make this house a haven and fill it with our children. How long do I have to wait before you think I'm ready? Don't I seem stable enough to handle it? It's been nearly eight months since . . . since . . . ;" she willed herself to say the words without flinching, "the last time; since the miscarriage."

"Sandy."

"Well, sometimes I get the feeling that you don't care if we never have a baby!"

She grimaced, shaking her head.

"I'm sorry, Peter. I didn't really mean that. I wish we could sit and talk about it; really explain our feelings to each other. Maybe we'd find out we're both ready."

"We will," he said, soothing her. "Very soon. Maybe in a couple of days, when I've whittled this pile down a little."

"I'll help you! Couldn't I do some of the basic stuff? Weed out the books that don't have something meaty on the subject, bracket the good passages in the others? I can read, you know!"

She stopped, hearing herself. "What am I doing?" She shook her head. "I never used to have such wild mood swings!"

"You're only upset because it's a subject you feel deeply about."

"I should be able to discuss it rationally. I should have some objectivity. But I get so emotional. . . ." She blinked and wiped her eyes. "You're right; we'll discuss it in a few days. And when we do, I'll be calmer; much, much calmer."

She watched as Peter set up a card table in the corner, put a blue chalk pencil and a pad of note paper in a small cardboard box, and stuck a hi-intensity lamp on the filing cabinet nearby.

"How's that for a temporary workspace?"

"It's fine. I'll be very good, and very quiet. When shall I start?"

"Well, mornings are bad. I need those to myself. Couldn't you give me a couple of hours right after lunch each day? I'll show you how I scan these: index and illustrations, then chapter skimming if it's warranted. You could save me some tedious digging if you really want to."

"I think you just bought yourself a research assistant," Sandy said. "It's really exciting, Peter. I think I'll be good at it!"

He pushed one pile of books over to her table. "The proof of the pudding, my dear. . . ."

"Oh, lord!" Sandy jumped to her feet. "What am I thinking of? You must he starved!"

"Now that you mention it. . . ."

She caught his hand. "You talk to me while I dress the salad."

"I'll put the coffee on."

"Aren't we lucky?" Sandy slipped her arm through his. "You've got a research assistant and I've got a kitchen helper."

They walked down the dim hall that led to the kitchen and dining room. The early evening air drenched the house with June smells; lilac and sweet grass, salt water, and something else, something heavy and musk-like that stirred the senses.

In the moment before they stepped into the lighted kitchen, Sandy felt a faint touch just below her ear, as if a warm mouth had breathed there and turned away.

She squeezed Peter's hand. Why couldn't she say what she felt without fear of being thought irrational or desperate?

"I love June," she said. It wasn't what she'd meant to say at all.

She started researching for him the next afternoon. She found it fascinating. "Sure you aren't bored?" Peter asked, over his glasses. "It's pretty dry and dusty stuff, unless you dig entymology. But the more I can condense it, the more conscise I am, the more interesting and readable it will be."

"Well, to tell you the truth," Sandy laughed, "I might be bored, if it weren't for my boss. Bugs aren't my favorite subject, but live and let live, I say."

Actually, she found the work absorbing. For months, there had been so little to stimulate her mental machinery. She could appreciate and respect Peter's efficient research method, so logical and easy to follow, and there were moments when the subject itself intruded on the mechanics of the job and really aroused her interest.

"Did you know," she asked, "that over fifty new species of moths have been found on the Galapagos Islands?"

"Interesting," Peter said, absorbed in his own reading.

Sandy stared at him soberly. If a show of initiative was what he wanted, initiative was what he'd get. She scanned and skimmed silently, blue-pencilled passages, put markers in the pages, and looked up after two hours to see Peter looking at her with a bemused expression.

"You don't keep good help by working them to death," he said. "Scram. Dismissed."

Sandy stretched, rubbing her neck. "That really does make the afternoon fly by!" She looked toward the window. "I think I'll take a walk."

"Good idea." Peter turned back to his work.

She glanced at herself in the hall mirror as she went out. The color in her face was becoming. A few strands of hair had fallen from her customary top knot to lie softly on her temples and ears. The effect was pretty in a gentle, undramatic way.

"Racquel Welch I'm not," Sandy said to her reflection. "But I've got a nice smile." She grinned to prove it. She felt good. Oh, helping Peter had made her feel good!

There was a windless hush over the island. It was reflected in the glassy surface of the sea. The air seemed oppressive, so still, so heavily scented. More of that strange, musky scent than yesterday.

Sandy set out for the woods. Perhaps it was cooler there. In the dark chambers under the trees, she walked through a pseudo-twilight where sounds intruded only dimly.

But here, too, the scent of musk lay heavy on the air, its effect almost soporific. She walked soundlessly on a carpet of needles inches deep, hearing a woodpecker somewhere close by, the ecstatic song of a thrush, quickly stilled, and a distant thrumming she couldn't identify.

The path was as familiar as her own house. She had walked it countless times as a child, less often as a woman. But she knew exactly where it dipped and turned; where the windfalls blocked it and had been chopped away; where a little stream ran full in June, dry in August.

As she approached the brook, the growth of spruce thinned, giving place to aspen and larch. Sunlight filtered down dappling the rocks, setting kaleidoscopic patterns in motion on the running water.

Sandy sat down on a mossy rock, with her back against a fallen tree. Behind her the forest was still and dark. The brook flowed endlessly past, its repeated pattern mesmerizing her. She sank back and closed her eyes. How easy it would be, she thought, to sleep; to just drift away on the warmth, the water, the rich dark smell of the trees.

The thrumming seemed to be all around her. She knew she was awake; she could feel the sun on her hand. But her eyes were so heavy. They refused to open, and she wanted so much to see what the thrumming was!

She stretched out her hand and felt the striated bark of a giant spruce. The thrumming was softer now, and she could hear a faint chittering sound, a whispering unlike anything she had ever heard.

She was floating, gliding, as helpless as a leaf on a stream.

Something very soft brushed her hand. She recoiled instinctively. She felt the hair lift from her ears, then fall gently against her temples. A feather trembled on her eyes and was suddenly gone. The touch freed her.

She opened her eyes upon a convocation of wings. A solid mass, layered on every rock, every twig, all in motion, beating in a sustained rhythm. The woods were alive with them, a seething carpet of pale moths.

Somehow, she knew that she was the focus of their excitement; a small island in their center, surrounded by two feet of clear ground, like an empty vortex in a whirlpool.

In their frenzy, they continually emitted the strange musk that made Sandy's head swim. Even as she stared at them in awe-struck fascination, she wondered why she felt no fear.

There was something almost musical in the hum of their wings, a sound of jubilation, of praise. They reminded her of worshippers, ecstatic before the object of their adoration.

Sandy felt an answering vibration on her breast. She tried to focus her eyes, but they kept slipping out of focus. There was something there, something centered exactly on her breastbone, but she couldn't overcome the lethargy that drugged her senses.

She felt herself spiralling down, down, back to the deep carpet of the forest floor, back out of the darkness into shifting light.

Silence and a freshening breeze restored her. She stared at the rocks, the tree trunks; at her own breast. There was nothing there. She felt like a dreamer, for whom the dream has been too real.

Her whole being declared what she knew to be true. She had not slept. She had not lost consciousness. In fact, she realized with a sudden leap of excitement, she had never felt more alive, more aware.

Her consciousness of life seemed heightened by the strange experience through which she had just passed.

She stood up.

Somewhere, just out of sight, a bird began a territorial plaint, rippling cascades that informed all intruders just where his boundaries lay.

He subsided when she walked back toward the house; but the woods were full of other sounds, all usual, all familiar.

She went straight to the study.

Absorbed, Peter was bent over the drawing table, his hair, too long uncut, bunching thickly over his collar.

She spoke his name softly.

If he heard her, he made no sign. His hunched shoulders shut her out as effectively as a wall.

"Peter!" she said.

He stirred slightly, his concentration broken, and turned a distant face toward her.

When he saw her strained and shadowed eyes, he stood up and walked toward her, his tension melting.

"What is it, Sandy?"

She stood with her back against the door frame, staring at him.

"Have I been hallucinating? No. It really happened."

"What happened?" He drew her to a chair and pulled his footstool up in front of her.

"Will you just listen and let me tell you, without any questions until I've finished? It's like remembering something out of a dream."

Peter took her hands in his, nodding.

She told him what she had felt and smelled and heard in the woods, until she had opened her eyes and seen the millions of wings.

"And I was in the center of them, suspended in space, and Peter, all their energy seemed focussed on me."

Peter reached out and touched her breast with his forefinger. It came away covered with a pale dust that emitted a musk-like fragrance.

"What is it?" Sandy whispered.

Peter looked at his fingertip, fascinated. "That's moth dust. If you felt something on your breast, it must have been the leader, the one they follow and obey. That's why they surrounded you in the woods."

Sandy fell against him, clutching his arms.

"Oh, Peter, then you do believe me!"

"Of course I believe you." He held her close. "You haven't exactly been babbling, you know. You told it all very logically and clearly, and it conforms to certain known patterns of behavior among some species. You may be a little shaky, but you're not out of your head!"

"But what are they doing, and what does it mean?"

"It could be a prelude to diapause," Peter said, rubbing the dust between his fingers. "Humans aren't usually privileged to see anything so fascinating, so strong."

"I think I've seen enough," Sandy said. "I wasn't exactly a clinical observer, you know. Those creatures were involving me in some mystical way and I could feel their...;" she frowned, reaching for the word that would describe what she felt, "...their intelligence, Peter. There was a focus there that could only be a mind!"

She stopped, staring at him.

"What is diapause?" she asked.

"It's a pause, sort of a biological marking time, before certain species change or progress into another stage of development. If that's what's happening, we may not see any activity for several days."

"But they'll still be here, around us?"

"Maybe not. They might move. But I have to doubt it. I expect they'll just subside now into a sort of inertia."

He sniffed the musky scent on his fingertips.

"You know, what you said about intelligence, that's pretty close to the mark. Migrating creatures do seem to move at the bidding of some mass consciousness. It's a fascinating concept."

"In theory, I suppose it is. In fact, I'd rather keep it in a textbook." She shivered and pressed herself into Peter's arms. "I wasn't exactly frightened, but it was really strange, really . . . eerie."

Peter made no reply. He rocked her gently in his arms, his eyes narrowed against the late sun through the western window. Musk sifted into his nostrils.

"That's pretty potent stuff; it's never going to replace Chanel Number Five."

"It makes me dizzy," Sandy said, "sort of disoriented." She looked up at him. "Does it affect you that way?"

"It affects me," Peter said. His voice was strangely flat and unfamiliar.

He went on quietly rocking her.

During the night, the wind shifted into the northeast, blowing hard. The sea built up before it, crashing ashore in one sustained roar. Rain began toward morning, adding to the sound and fury, isolating the point where the house stood.

Sandy slept restlessly. The clicks and tappings of the rain stitched uneasy sound across her dreams. Behind it, the unbroken roar of the sea shook the shore and filled the heavens, like a great unchained beast.

She got up twice and went to the window.

Peter didn't stir.

In the morning, he woke early to a grey drizzle in the passing storm. "Why were you up in the night?"

Sandy rolled toward him. "You were awake? Why didn't you say something?"

"I was going to speak, but I wasn't sure you'd welcome my intruding on your thoughts."

"Didn't the storm make you uneasy?"

"It has some kind of reverse effect on me, I think. The wilder it gets, the more snug and secure I feel in here."

Sandy shivered. "I don't feel as if I'd slept at all."

"So go to sleep now. It's quieter. And it's early, only six forty-five."

"Okay." She turned away and moved back against him, spoon-fashion, curling into his body with a sigh.

"Peter."

"I thought you were going to sleep."

"Do you think they've gone? Did the storm blow them away?"

"Maybe." His voice sounded distant. "Even if they're still on this peninsula, we may never see them again. Go to sleep."

She did.

Rough seas continued for several days, and Peter postponed his trip to the mainland.

"We've got plenty of material here," he said. "It will be a week or more before you have this stuff digested into notes for me, and I'm still doing research on physical detail for the illustrations in this chapter." He rubbed his eyes.

Sandy looked up from her post at the card table. "You look tired."

Peter stretched, rubbing his neck. "I could use a break. How about you?"

"In a minute."

He went down the hall to the kitchen. Sandy could hear him open the refrigerator, then a moment later the back door slammed.

She finished making a notation, stuck it in the book she was scanning and closed the cover.

The house was very still.

Peter had left one of his brushes on the edge of his drawing table. It rolled down suddenly and brought up in the pencil tray.

Sandy went over to look at the drawings Peter had completed during the morning.

A series of pen and ink sketches depicted the larval stages of the moth. One partially finished water color showed a species with white-rimmed black spots on extended wings like two intent staring eyes. There was another painting tacked to the far right edge of the table. Sandy recognized it as the painting of a leaf she had first seen nearly a week before.

The leaf was ugly. She stared at it. Where in nature was there a green like that? The leaf seemed larger than she remembered it, more full and swollen, as if the cocoon inside were ready to burst.

Had Peter altered it?

"I'll just find him and ask him," she said, tearing her gaze from the image which both fascinated and frightened her.

She went out the side door, along the edge of the terrace to the rugged shore path. From the top of it she could see clearly in both directions. Peter was nowhere in sight.

The wind had diminished, and on the long ocean swells gulls were riding sedately, turning their heads this way and that, with dignified curiosity.

Sandy walked back around the house to the woods path. She hesitated at the edge of the back yard, just where the narrow track plunged into the shadow of the trees.

How dark it seemed, after the sunlit glare of the ocean! A tunnel, a pit, full of unseen rustlings and stirrings, always just ahead or behind, always just out of sight.

Slowly her eyes adjusted to the lack of light. The feeling of menace vanished. It was a woodland path, nothing more.

She walked in.

A plover rose from the brush, fluttered ahead of her a few feet and settled to earth. As she approached, it repeated the performance, its panic flight a graceless comedy.

Where the path turned toward the brook, she saw Peter's footprint in the rain-soaked earth. Water was seeping into it.

"Peter!" she called. "Where are you?"

She came out into the partial sunlight along the bank of the stream. It raced along in full voice, swollen with rain.

Sandy looked about her. It seemed useless to shout; the water made so much noise. She searched for some sign, another footprint, and suddenly, she saw him.

He was standing on the lichen-clad trunk of a fallen spruce, motionless, his head thrown back, staring up into the trees.

His trance-like attitude frightened her. She stepped toward him cautiously, and reached out.

"Peter?"

"Go back," he said, unmoving.

"Peter!"

"They're here. They're still here."

He hadn't moved. His eyes were riveted on something unseen. But his voice, low and urgent, carried across the few feet that separated them with almost physical force.

Sandy stood rooted to the spot. Was there danger she was unaware of? Something Peter had deliberately kept from her?

During her encounter with the creatures she had felt no real fear. What had happened to make Peter behave so strangely?

"You come, too!" she said.

"Soon."

"Why is it bad for me to stay, but all right for you?"

"The entire mass is moving, changing, alive with some tremendous common energy, as if they . . . as if *it* had a single purpose. I don't know what it means, but I intend to find out."

"Peter. . . ."

"Go home, Sandy," he whispered fiercely. "If I remain motionless, silent, I may witness something no one else has ever seen."

"I won't leave! Let me stay! I'll be very still, I promise."

She took Peter's silence as assent, and moved back to the log on the stream bank. There she could stand with her back to the light, looking deep into the green shade where he stood like a statue. The space beneath the trees began to glow in reflected energy. Phosphorescence glittered on tree trunks and roots. Pine needles were bathed in it. Peter's upturned face shone waxy white, and his eyebrows sparkled.

The brightness grew, pressing down from above with blinding intensity. Sandy wanted to run, wanted to yell, wanted to pull Peter away from that descending power, but her eyes rebelled against the brilliance, and she covered them with her hands, helpless against the inertia she felt. The smell of musk was overpowering.

Peter was a figure in a dream, suspended above the ground in a halo of light, turning, turning in a sheath of green silk, round and round until he was a tightly wrapped cocoon that glowed with energy.

Sandy struggled to move, to shake off the spell in which she seemed frozen. She wanted to reach Peter, to tear that vile covering from his slowly revolving body, fixed in space; she wanted to run, to find clear, fresh air to breathe; she wanted more than anything, to wake up!

She felt, rather than saw, a shadow deep as a cloud pass low overhead, darkening the sun. In that instant she could breathe, speak, move, and she leaped to her feet, her heart hammering.

Peter was coming toward her, only the expression in his eyes betraying his feelings. He appeared perfectly normal.

Sandy flung herself at him.

"Oh, Peter," she alternately clutched him and thrust him away to stare into his face. "Are you all right? What happened to you?"

"Nothing! I feel wonderful; but for a while there, I felt as if. . . ." He frowned. "I wasn't asleep, I wasn't unconscious. . . ."

"I saw you!" Sandy cried. "You were hanging in the air, you were spinning round and round! Oh, Peter, they were spinning a cocoon around you, a shining silk, all green. . . ."

"No, no," he laughed shakily, "I never moved from that spot; I was perfectly aware, Sandy, but I couldn't budge; I was enchanted! Did you see that phosphorescence? They produced that by a force of will, and all the while the dust showered down, dry and sweet."

"You *moved*!" Sandy whispered. "Peter, you were up in the air. That's how I felt when they came to me, as if I were raised up through no effort of my own, raised to them by some unseen force. And I felt wonderful afterward, so alive, as if the world were new!"

"You were hallucinating; it's the dust, so musky and sweet, it alters consciousness to some degree. I never moved, Sandy, and neither did you. But we did blunder into some momentous transition ritual of theirs. Who'd believe they could produce that light, so concentrated, so. . . ."

"Focussed?" Sandy breathed. "Focussed, Peter, on you." She pulled at him. "Let's go now." She began to run.

He hurried after her.

"Wait! Don't run! There's nothing to fear!" He caught her arm, slowing her wild plunge along the sodden track.

"Look, Sandy, that focus is the mind you talked about after you saw them; it's the power that generates the light. It's like pure mental energy. It's an astounding phenomenon, but it's not a menace!"

They came out of the woods into the June sunlight.

Sandy turned to face him.

"What is happening, then. If it's not us who's being moved, or changed, or used, then what is happening?"

"They are in the middle of some new evolutionary step, and every one of them is a cell in the mind that's governing the change. They can't be distracted, they can't be deterred, until it's accomplished. There must be millions of them."

He faced her in the sunlight, and she gasped.

From head to foot, he shimmered and glowed with an unearthly light. Dust drifted from his hair, his clothes, his fingers.

"Look at yourself," Sandy said, covering her nose, "and smell yourself!"

Peter raised his hand and examined it, then brushed futilely at his clothes. He breathed the musk-cloud that surrounded him, and his eyes dilated, glittering. For a moment he was motionless. Then he smiled. "I like it," he said.

Sandy shivered. His smile seemed grotesque, distorted.

But he shed his clothes at the side door, and washed himself under the lawn hose, gasping at the cold.

Sandy brought him a towel and his terry robe and stood by unhappily as he rubbed himself dry. The lowering sun was warm, but she shivered uncontrollably, and her knees felt as boneless as Jello. She knew it was a reaction, slightly delayed, but the knowledge did nothing to firm up her rubbery legs.

She sat down abruptly on the porch steps. Peter sank down beside her, smelling pleasantly damp and familiar.

"It's over, you know. It was a pretty awesome spectacle, but it's really over. They're gone. The transition or evolution, whatever it was they were experiencing, is complete and they've moved on."

"They darkened the sun," Sandy said, remembering.

"It's nothing scientists haven't recorded before, that kind of mass movement. Even in the Bible, the swarms of locusts, mass migration of a species. Same thing. But my God, it's exciting, isn't it?"

"Have scientists ever recorded that concentration of energy, the light, the *mind* in that swarm?"

"Nothing documented. Only some theories, some speculations." Peter shook his head. "Being there, seeing it, makes you feel part of something almost cosmic."

"Let's go in," Sandy said, pulling his arms around her. "I'm exhausted, and cold. Will you build a fire? And I'll fix something for supper."

After supper, she sat close to the fire, while Peter wrote feverishly, making pencilled notes of all the aspects of his experience. His absorption excluded her. She picked up her mug of tea, and wandered into the study.

She snapped on Peter's working light, and saw the drawing she had intended to ask him about in the afternoon. Stunned, unbelieving, she bent over it.

The leaf was open; it's edges torn and ragged, its interior a silky translucent green. It almost filled the paper. The tiny guardian moths were nowhere to be seen.

Sandy stared at it, panic rising in suffocating waves.

"Peter!" she called. "Come here!"

"Can't you wait a minute?" he asked. "I'm really rolling on this, and I'd like to finish."

"No!" she said, and began to cry stormily. "I can't wait! Something is crazy about this, and I want to know. . . ."

He came running.

She pointed at the picture of the leaf, so exquisitely done, so real.

Peter frowned. "What, Sandy? The leaf drawing? What about it?" He looked genuinely perplexed.

"It's changed!" she screamed at him. "Can't you see that?"

"Don't. Don't do this. You've been doing so well! Sandy, look, calm down!" He tried to take her in his arms, but she twisted away from him.

"It was a small, ugly thing, all curled up, and then bigger, with a cocoon inside, and now it's empty, dead and empty, and huge."

Peter's hands caught at her arms and held them fast.

"It's a tenant leaf, empty after metamorphosis, just the way I drew it, and you are just completely overwrought, and imagining things."

"No," Sandy said softly. "No."

"I'm putting you to bed, Sandy. You've got to rest, really let go and rest. In the morning you'll feel like a new person, you'll know they've really gone, and we've just been two of the privileged few who've been witnesses to a natural phenomenon."

While he spoke, he was carrying her down the hall, cradled against his chest, and she was so tired, so tired, and the familiar warmth of him was so reassuring. Like a tired child, she closed her eyes and fell asleep as soon as her head touched the pillow, conscious of Peter's body stretched out protectively beside her.

In the night, she awoke to the smell of musk, oppressively near. "Peter?" she said sleepily, putting out her hand.

She felt him draw closer, felt the bed tremble under the shift of his weight, and turned to meet him, with a tired sigh.

In the darkness she was enfolded, tenderly, by a giant wing.

Pat Crossman was born on Vinalhaven, grew up and went to school in Massachusetts, but returned every summer to the island. Her family lived there from 1789, and she returned to stay in 1948. "Moths" is Crossman's second story to be included in a collection of short stories. She is now working on a novel which has the Maine coast as its locale.

The novel, Freeman Cooper, *was privately published in 1971 by the late William Hopkins of North Haven. Hopkins, an English teacher, fisherman, mariner, and local philosopher, was born on North Haven in 1924 and died in 1979.*

Freeman Cooper, *although not widely known in Maine or elsewhere, did attract the attention of Columbia University's English Professor Mark Van Doren. Van Doren wrote, "It's a very funny, very serious book. Its dialogue comes with gale force out of people whom the author has realized with perfect freedom and frankness. I have seldom so enjoyed any book."*

Freeman Cooper *paints, in rich detail, the story of a Maine island's native son who confronts the death of his mother and his subsequent attempt to come to terms with his ambivalent attitudes about island life during a bleak winter. In this excerpt we find Freeman Cooper discussing everything under the sun with some neighbors in the store down at the harbor.*

. . .

44

Freeman Cooper

(Excerpt from a Novel)

William R. Hopkins

A fter I left Manetta's, I went back to the store.
The stormy crowd was there. All of them. They had all been there, off and on, for a week. There is so little to do in such a blizzard of long standing, and you can soon get sick of sitting around your own house with nothing to do.

It is a good thing to have the store at such times.

Lucy was taking Bebe's place in the store, as clerk. . . .

They did not stop talking when I went in, so I knew they had not been talking about me, which was a relief, in a way.

They were mostly natives; the foreigners do not hang around the store much. They know where they are not wanted — all except Buddy Swipes.

They seem to tolerate him, but then, he is not so bad, to talk to. . . .

He was there, in the store, in his place, but not talking.

He spoke to me; the others nodded, but did not interrupt or change their conversations.

Well, well, mah ol' Buddy Free. How are you this morning, ol' Buddy, Free?

Hi, Buddy. Cold. Hi, Stinky!

Cold? Hell! What you talkin' about, Captain. Anybody'd ought to gct a big barrel somewheres and make up a mint julep. Got plenty of ice. . . .

I suppose so. . . .

Ah 'spec we might. . . .

Hi, Free. Quite a day. This would be a good morning to breed somebody, wouldn't it?

One thing that gets me about these summer people that comes here: they got all the money in the United States Treasury behind them, and yet they buy that cheap, rot-gut whiskey.

Not a great while to town meeting.

Almost on us.

Mrs. Castlewood, up there on the hill: they buy up all that cheapest kind of stuff they can lay their hands onto and swill it down like tap water, six to eight ounces to a time. She give me a water glass full, one of them tall ones, once in a while, when I was working up there on the hill. I'd sit it under a bush somewhere and nip away on it 'till noon time.

They h'ain't much town meeting talk this time. You don't know what in hell's going on. . . .

That old Mrs. Castlewood. She come up to my house one time. She's pleasant. She likcd the looks of my place. She said she thought I had the prettiest spot in the world. I told her summers was all right but the winters was something shocking, and she says: they are? I can't believe it. I think this must be a perfectly darling place in the winter! I wish, by God, she could see it now. She'd take one look at that white devil-shit drove clear to the eaves on the no'th'east side, where the wind curls right between the house and the barn, and I bet she'd think it was quite darlin' now all right!

That Mrs. Castlewood, I remember the time Marland told her about the deer over to Isle au Haut. He said they were standing so thick on the shore, coming up under the land from outside at night, that their eyes lit up like Revere Beach when everything's going. . . .

That Marland. He feeling any better?

No, sir. The goddamn fool.

H'ain't had his gall bladder cut out yet. . . .

No, the damned fool. I told Ma last summer when he had that bad attack and we tried to get him to go into the hospital, I said: No, Ma. Don't urge him no more. What he's going to do is he's going to wait 'till the snow's right to the top of them windows, then he's going to have a goddamn ringer of an attack just so's we'll all bust our guts getting him out to the hospital, and I guess, by God, I was right. He's in the middle of a siege right now. I hit him on it this morning. I says: there, goddam ya! Lay right there and suffer! You had your chance last summer! He knows what I meant. He don't say nothin' to me no more. He knows better.

Too bad to let him suffer.

Well, I don't feel sorry for him, even if he is my own son. . . .

Someone said you were running for First, Free, that right?

I've thought some about it.

Well, either you be or you be'nt. I should think you'd let us know one way or the other so's we'd see what we could do about getting you enough votes.

I think I will.

You think! Don't you know?

Yes. I know.

Well, there!

Well, it h'ain't only gall bladders today. They's gall bladders, yes, and they's lots of other real sickness, but most of that you don't have to worry much about because the doctors can fix it. They can snap out a gall bladder or they can whip out your appendixes, and it h'ain't no more trouble than snippin' off a wen. But the ones they can't seem to do nothin' about — not countin' the killin'-ones like cancers and that stuff — is the millions of people that is unwell but they h'ain't really sick yet. . . .

What th'hell are you talkin' about, Az? You supposed to be a doctor, or something?

No. I h'ain't no doctor. But I got eyes, and I got brains, h'ain't I?

Well, your eyes h'ain't too good. You wear glasses, I notice. And I don't know what in hell you got for brains, but it don't make much sense talkin' about millions of people that is unwell but they h'ain't really sick yet. . . .

It does too. They's millions of 'em.

Who, for instance?

Take somebody like yourself. You smoke a pile of cigarettes a day and you're hackin' on phlegm all day. Every morning you wake up and you feel like a shag shit in your mouth — takes you twenty-five minutes to get your feet braced every morning. But you don't stop smokin'! You could throw away your cigarettes and in ten days' time you could feel human. But you don't do it. They h'ain't no doctor knows what to do about that. Same thing with my brother Bossie: He wakes up in the mornin' and starts right in drivin' the coffee to him. He drinks a dozen cups a day; he h'ain't never more than twenty minutes away from a cup of hot coffee. So he goes around peltin' the Roll-Aids to himself all day and his old guts feels like a forest fire and he's burpin' and fartin' himelf to death by inches. He could leave the coffee alone for a whole week and his guts would normal out, his nerves would settle down, and he'd probably even stop pickin' his nose all the time. But he doesn't do it. No doctor can't make him do it neither. You fellers is just like better'n half the population today. You're unwell, but you h'ain't sick enough to stop doing what you're doing wrong. Someday you will be. Probably you'll strangle to death with a lung cancer and my brother Bossie will end up havin' to have half his gut cut out and thrown away and starve to death on Malox and baby food.

Well, that's all settled, then. You going to run, Free, and you h'ain't going to back out on us.

I am going to run. . . .

That's all we need to know. But, by God, you got to cut out these all-night parties. You know that. Jesus Christ! It don't help none with them church people to have 'em carrying horny women out of your house feet first every morning. . . .

It only happened once; it was an accident. . . .

Accident be damned! She just got crocked, that's all. And from what I hear, I guess it weren't the first time. That don't go over too good around here — if you're looking for votes — and I suppose you are. . . .

Ma says, well, everybody's been trying to get Marland to go to the hospital, but I guess he's part mule. I don't know who he takes after! And I says: I guess you'd better take a look in the looking glass to see who he takes after. . . .

You talk about stubborn! When I was steamboatin', I fell in with a damn bastard that turned out to be an outlaw. I lived with him two weeks down to Virginia Beach. . . .

Why h'ain't you took the time to tell us you was runnin'. . . .

I have to bury Mother first.

I 'spec you must. It's going to be a bad one. They got the grave open yet?

They're still working.

They working today, in this?
They're doing all they can.
Well, we'll have to put it off. You'll have to put it off 'till the snow stops, Free.
You can wait just so long. . . .
I know, another day or two. This will let up bim'by. They bringing her today?
This afternoon.
I s'pose she'll go right to the church. Proper thing.
It will be easier.
No point in going to the house. She'll be all right at the church until we can have the service.
When d'you plan, Tuesday?
Tuesday afternoon. Two o'clock.
Most of us has our flowers coming tonight. We couldn't wait too long. But they'll keep for a while up there in the cellars to the church.
Susie was telling that most of us has ordered the pinks. We know what the plants will do this time of the year. But Etta told that most of the foreigners has ordered plants, the damned fools. Wouldn't you suppose they'd know by now plants freeze?
You don't give a plant no chance to set it on a grave this time a'year. But, then, most of them bastards don't know nothin' and most of them never will.
Well, you got to have good courage, Free. You lucky enough to get into town office and things are going to be tough. They's going to be somebody on your ass every day in the week.
Yessir, Free. You want to be braced to be criticized every time you turn around. They'll criticize everything you do — and some things you don't.
Just remember Aunt Eunice, though, Free. Aunt Eunice always said criticism takes from the tree caterpillars and blossoms together. . . .
Well, I don't know so much about that either, Free. Old Doc, there, he's pretty smart sometimes. And he says a man can't neither protect nor defend himself against criticism, so he's just got to act in spite of it and sooner or later, by Jesus, it will gradually give in to him. . . .
That may be true in some places, but around here. . . .
You remember that time George Young tried to run the turnip farm?
Who?
George Young. He had something to say about getting criticized. . . .

Broke his arm?

No. Tried to run the turnip farm. . . .

I remember George Young.

You remember George Wooster?

George Lewis? Yes. I remember him too. . . .

For chrissakes, Granpa, turn up your h'arkin' iron. . . .

Turnips what?

Turn up your hearing aid!

'T won't do no good. She's been buzzin' lately. I guess she's broke.

Well, you give 'em hell, Free. You make it, you give 'em hell. We'll all stand behind you. Anything to get rid of old Bossie Gray and that goddamn wife of his. That Lizzie, she's the one. She's the one that runs the town. You couldn't shut her up if you clapped a rat trap right over her goddamn beak. . . .

My brother Bossie, he poisons minds too. . . .

I guess that h'ain't all he poisons. . . .

That Lizzie. I guess she got her comeuppance that time last summer when her sister that married that goddam Lunt from the east'ard sent that foolish kid of hers up here for Lizzie to take care of....

Oh, you mean that Wilbur? He was a dream.

Yeah. That was the kid that ate the toothpaste, wasn't it?

I guess he did. He was half starved, besides being half foolish. I guess he ate a whole tube of it between Friday afternoon and Monday morning 'fore they finally got rid of him and sent him back. Every time they'd lose track of him, they'd find him up in the bathroom driving the toothpaste to himelf. He was half foolish.

You'd think so if you ever saw that old man of his. He's about one brick short of a load. You ever see him?

Don't think ever I did.

Jees. He was working down there to the shipyard that year I sailed for the Judge. We was in there one time and that kid's old man came down aboard with another feller to make a screen for the hatch. The old Judge lost one of the screens overboard in the night. Well, that other feller didn't quite have all his marbles either, and they were struggling with the measurements and that old Lunt, there, he looked up to me with those old buck teeth aimed right at me, and he says: Buh! We make an awful good team. He makes all the marks and I rub 'em out. Jees, he was a dream. . . .

He must'a been a lot like that old Irishman that was visiting down to Magmadlin's mother's that summer. He thought he was quite a mechanic, and them summer kids showed up with that outboard motor they'd been foolin' around with. He looked her over and they asked him if he could fix it, and he said he didn't know, he'd have to think about it, and finally he says: Ah, Lads, this thinkin' makes the head ache; you'd better take her somewheres else. . . .

That's what you're going to be up against, Free. You going to have to be thinking all the time, you get into office. But they h'ain't no sense to worry. You may not even make it. . . .

I wouldn't want to run and not make it.

That's politics, Free.

I wouldn't want to do it.

Don't worry, Free. You run; we'll see to it you get in. But they h'ain't too many of us left. You better butter up some of those outlandishmen too. . . .

To hell with the outlandishmen, Free. I'd just as liv see them run a candidate of their own. I'd like to see what would happen. I don't believe they got the strength they think they have. It's time we had a showdown and found out whether they going to take the town away from us or not. If they h'ain't, by God, they better pull their asses into the corner and shut up. If they be, then it's time for all us decent folks to move out. I say let's have a showdown and settle it. . . .

You want to be careful, George. They just might take us. They's more and more of 'em every year. . . .

I say they can't do it. Blood is thicker'n water, and. . . .

It h'ain't blood; it's votes. I'd be a'feared they'd have 'em. . . .

I h'ain't a'feared of nothin'. Them bastards h'ain't took us over yet, and by God, they h'ain't about to. . . .

For myself, I do not care to think about it.

I had heard all I needed to at the store.

I had given them something to think about. They would have to talk it over. Everyone would want his say, now that it was out in the open. They would not want to talk about it with me there. It was almost time for noon meal anyway with Aunt Lena and Uncle Cy.

I came away.

William Hopkins was born on North Haven Island in Penobscot Bay in 1924. Following four years in the Navy as a submariner during World War II, he attended the University of Maine. Besides teaching on North Haven and Vinalhaven, and in Rockland and Orono, Maine, he was a party fishing boat operator, a ferry boat captain, a licensed pilot, real estate broker, census-taker, and a Justice of the Peace. He was married and had five sons.

In addition to his novel, *Freeman Cooper*, letters that Bill Hopkins wrote during the last year of his life were published in the book, *Better Than Dying*. These letters revealed his enthusiasm for life and optimism during his cancer ordeal. He died in 1979.

A Family Dinner

(Excerpt from a Novel in Progress)

Emily Muir

For the first time since the war the family was all together again. They were lucky ones with both boys home again and no missing limbs, though it had been a close call for Willy, in the water eight hours before being picked up. Bessie had prayed every day for her children, but others had prayed too, church folk and folk who never saw the inside of a church, and many of their children never came home.

Martha had arranged her visit to coincide with Reeder's leave, and Bessie had killed two fat hens, plucked and roasted them till the skins were a crisp golden brown. In the center of the red and white checked table cloth they sat on platters, stuffing bursting from their brown skins.

Until she smelled the chickens cooking Martha had forgotten how good food could taste. Restaurant chicken wasn't much to brag of — the kind of restaurants she and Bart ate in — and you couldn't roast a bird on a hot plate in the bathroom. Her parents of course were countrified folk, stuck away on an island off the Maine coast, but Ma knew how to cook, she had to admit. She ought to have learned from her when she was growing up but she was a rebel — had always been a rebel — resentful of the role conferred on women by fate. She had told her mother:

"All you think a woman is good for is dishing up three meals a day, and having babies like rabbits."

She was the eldest and yet she had always to play second fiddle to Willy. Willy and Reeder could go to a hop and ask any girl they wanted, though Willy was too clumsy to dance, but she had to sit on the sidelines and wait to be asked. It was still a man's world and like to stay that way until women got together and decided to do something about it.

A woman here on the island was expected to stay home, but the government had trained her as a secretary and she had a well-paying job in San Francisco with Peckham Jones and Griffin. Yet she had to admit there had been times when the walls of the corporation seemed to close in on her, and she would find herself thinking of the knoll overlooking the harbor, of this kitchen with the family gathered around the table, and the thought had left such an emptiness in her she had wanted to grab her things and catch the first plane home. When the fog came drifting in through the Golden Gate and she would button up her overcoat to keep warm, she would remember the kitchen stove radiating its heat and the smell of bread baking in the oven; see Gilbert asleep in the rocker, paws curled over his nose; and hear the suck-squeek, suck-squeek of the pump in the kitchen sink.

Ever since she could remember, water had been piped into the milk room in the barn for Pa's precious cows, but not even Ma's persistent nagging had gotten it as far as the kitchen sink. As for hot water, it had to be dipped from the reservoir alongside the stove. How could anyone live without a bathroom in 1955? It was bad enough having to use the outhouse with its cold drafts and smell of lime, but however was she going to manage a bath in the old tin tub?

Sitting at table Martha found it difficult to think she grew up in such a pokey little place. With the granite quarry shut down and the steamboats gone it was even deader than it was before. All her friends had either left the island like herself or become stodgy housewives with half a dozen kids clinging to their skirts. She had no inclination for marriage, yet she had to admit a man and a woman needed each other. So she and Bart had taken an apartment together in San Francisco. Fortunately there were ways to avoid having babies.

Back and forth her thoughts flew across the continent, but with the first taste of chicken and Ma's cranberry jam, the berries picked from the bog by the pond, Martha was not so sure she liked her life on the West Coast, with Bart there one night and gone the next, and herself never quite sure these were the business trips he claimed they were. True he told her often enough she was as beautiful as a girl of sixteen, and studying her reflection in the mirror she felt he was not insincere. She had kept her figure, her hair curled naturally, her complexion was fresh and clear. Yet how could she be sure he didn't say these same words to another those nights when he was away "on business"? Once she had considered marrying him but of course that was wishful thinking. Marriage had never yet been a deterrent to a man and his affairs. Things were freer without marriage — but freer for what? For a man to sleep with his girlfriends? It was lonely in the one-room apartment with Bart gone.

Caught between two worlds in neither of which she wholly belonged, Martha realized, sitting in her mother's kitchen, that she was nearing thirty without the slightest idea what she wanted to do with her life.

She had that stuff on her lips, Bessie noticed, and no need of it with her high coloring. And those plucked eyebrows! Lord they ruined a girl's looks, clipped to a hair-line and darkened with pencil. She looked like a harlot. And Martha with fine dark eyebrows of her own! Wilmont had already expressed his feelings on the subject, but it made no difference to young folk these days what their parents thought. Martha did what she wanted — always had and always would. Living in sin with that man out there on the West Coast! She'd had half a mind to shut the door in her daughter's face, but Wilmont wouldn't hear of it.

"She's our daughter, Bessie," he'd said. "Whatever she's done we got to take some of the blame. Things are different these days from the way they was when we were yu'ones. They think we're nothing but a pair of old fogies lived beyond our time. Mind I don't admire what she's doing, but it ain't in me to think my daughter's wicked —leastwise not more'n most folk in this imperfect world."

The good Lord knew she'd tried to give her children a Christian upbringing, but the way things had turned out both girls had disgraced the family name.

At least she could take comfort in that Willy was properly married with a church wedding and all the trimmings. And there was her grandson, little Arnold, lying in his folding crib waving his arms, rolling his big blue eyes, blowing bubbles. And Hanna was expecting again.

Bessie leaned over and poked a finger into the baby's ribs, making foolish little sounds so that the baby opened his mouth, twisting it into something like a grin.

"He's smiling at Granny," she said. "Little Arnold is smiling at his granny."

"Nonsense," Martha replied, "it's just gas."

Martha had a way of spoiling people's pleasure as well as her own, Wilmont thought sadly. Not that she meant to, he supposed. It was just that she didn't seem to fit in anywhere, and it irked her to see others enjoying themselves.

Willy, built solid like his Pa, with a hearty appetite, helped himself liberally to potatoes and gravy. Ma knew how to feed men, he thought. He'd never say it to Hanna but Ma was a better cook than his wife would ever be. He loved Hanna — or so he supposed. Still he had thoughts that bothered him sometimes. It wasn't just the shock of the Kamikaze striking the ship and sending it to the bottom, the long hours in the water, or the beach strewn with bodies. These gave him nightmares, but in the daytime he kept thinking of Kyomi and her tantalizing black eyes, the small rosy lips like a red bud.

Until he met Kyomi he had thought of the Japs as monkeys, short, flat-nosed, oriental monkeys diving out of the sky. Even in their own country he had thought them ape-like, the women old and wrinkled, or young and simpering. Kyomi was different — illusive, lovely, with silken skin, warm and golden. It seemed he could never get enough of her. They had lived together for two strange and wonderful weeks, and though she gave herself to him freely, she had always seemed somehow just out of his reach so that he was never satisfied. Silent, partaking generously of the food, he saw her now in her blue flow-ered kimono running away from him with little mincing steps, calling over her shoulder, "Weely, Weely!" laughing, beckoning. But though he pursued her with all his long American legs, he was unable to catch up with her. And though he yearned to, he could never quite recapture the feel of her in his arms.

"Come on, snap out of it, Willy," Reeder said. "If I didn't know you, I'd think you had the belly ache."

Know me! Willy thought, you don't know me. Hell! I don't even know myself. Aloud he said nothing, but leaned over to look at the baby in the carryall. He was proud of his son, proud of Hanna with her beautiful blond hair. His mother said the expression that passed over the baby's face reminded her of him at that age. That was nonsense. All babies looked alike at that age, except maybe his looked older —more like a little boy. Arnold would grow into a boy, a real boy. He would take him fishing — make a fisherman out of him. They would fish together, father and son. With his son with him he would forget Kyomi. . . .

Reeder was wearing the old green sweater his Ma had knit for him years ago. Stretched taut across his shoulders it scarcely covered his belly, but he was wearing it for old time's sake, and Bessie had already measured him for another. His blue uniform hung behind the door in his old bedroom where Bessie had gone surreptitiously to finger the gold braid, saying to herself, "The youngest warrant officer in Com-munications," though this distinction was long out of date. Behind the door of his bedroom all his old clothes were hung neatly on the old hooks — jackets too tight in the chest, sleeves too short, pantlegs halfway up to his ankles, but all neatly washed and pressed, mended and brushed, awaiting his return. On the table his old sending set was just as he had left it, except for the aerial, which had blown down in the hurricane. He smiled, remembering his twelfth birthday when they had first given it to him. Pa wouldn't let him climb up on the barn roof.

"You'll get yourself kilt," Pa had insisted, climbing the ladder himself while Reeder had stood there watching his father's clumsy motions, calling out: "Watch it, Pa! Be careful!" half wishing his Pa would slip just to prove he could have done it better, and scared to death he would.

A sense of belonging stole over Reeder, who had traveled over half the face of the earth. It was home, an anchor firmly caught against the vicissitudes of a changing world. In Asia it seemed half the people were adrift without home or family, food or shelter. But it was no time to think such thoughts, with all the good food on the table and no way to share it with others. He swallowed the meat on his fork, helped himself to stuffing and gravy and smiled at his Ma.

"You sure know how to serve up a great mess of vittles, Ma. I sure wish we could sign you aboard as cook."

Bessie was pleased. "Gracious sakes, Reeder, you know very well all I got to do is set foot aboard a vessel tied up to the dock and my belly turns upside down. I ain't no sailor nor ever will be, and I never did see how you could take it, tossed around night and day on all those waves." She beamed proudly at him, thinking how clever this son was who understood things like radio and atom bombs.

There was something good and stable about the island, Reeder acknowledged. Still a place can't stay the same forever in a fast-changing world. When he retired with his pension, he'd come back and change a few things — schools — there were two high schools on one small island — medical services — there was only one doctor. There would be plenty for a retired man to do.

"The old place don't change much," he said.

"Hu! You don't live here," Willy reminded him. "The quarry shut down and every last man of 'em set out traps. There's more traps than lobsters."

"That's right," Reeder agreed. "There's nothing for a kid to do when he gets out of school but fish. So we're losing all our kids to Connecticut and Massachusetts. Up there they've got to compete with graduates from modern schools."

"*You* went to this school," Bessie snapped. "You done all right!"

"You can't get decent teachers to come to an old rundown school stuck away on an island," Martha cut in. "You ought to see the schools in San Francisco!"

"Maybe they've got money in San Francisco," Bessie tried to clinch the argument.

"You'd have a lot more money for improvement if there was one high school for both towns on this island. They ought to pool their resources."

They're right, Wilmont thought. We don't change. We live one day at a time, limping along, till our kids come back and trip us up. Aloud he said:

"Time was, this island was one town. They fought over taxes and now they can't cooperate on anything. A man marries and settles in the Landing and changes all his thinking. Nothing Boldwater does after that is right, and vice versa. I misdoubt you'll ever get the two towns together in one school."

Gladine, Wilmont and Bessie's youngest child, looked up from spooning gravy onto Davey's plate. "Sue Closson used to be our best cheerleader. She married that freak from the Landing and he comes to all the games to cheer for our team. It makes me furious."

Reeder looked at his sister. She was still nothing but a child and ought never to have married, poor kid. He said, "I guess I've got my work cut out for me when I retire."

"You meaning to come home when you get out of the Navy?" Wilmont asked, surprised.

"If Ma'll board me."

"I'll do nothing of the sort," Bessie declared. "You need a woman of your own, Reeder Clegg, a woman to take care of you, fat you up. Land sakes, you're skinny as a rail. It's that old food the Navy dishes up! Look at you, nigh on to thirty and not married. You don't aim to stay a bachelor all your life I should hope." It didn't seem possible that in another ten years or so he could retire. Most folk didn't retire till they were seventy and then some. Farmers and fishermen mostly died with their boots on. Still the idea of Reeder coming home was one to make her smile with pleasure. Some day she would have a little red-headed grandson to love and coddle.

"You got someone in mind?" he teased her.

"No, but give me a minute to think."

They were laughing at her now.

"Don't hurry, Ma. You've got plenty of time. It'll be a few years yet. First thing I mean to do when I get home is build a television set."

"A television set? What's that?"

"It's a small movie screen with sound you can set up in your own house so you can watch the Red Sox and the Yankees play sitting right in your chair."

"Humph!" Bessie said, "Next thing they'll have windows alongside the telephone so you can see your neighbor standing there in his underdrawers and the Lord only knows what else."

Wilmont looked around the table. His children were grown. Only yesterday they were babies, and in that yesterday the world was a different place. A man simply couldn't credit the changes that had taken place in his lifetime. He had been born in the horse and buggy age — and was like never to emerge from it his children thought —and now it was the atomic age. Reeder seemed to think atomic energy would be harnessed for peaceful purposes, but he was certain of one thing. Atomic energy would never have been discovered if it hadn't been for the war. The Germans were trying to break down the atom to blow up the Allies, but we got there first and used it on the Japs. If other countries got it — Lord, a man couldn't imagine a world full of atomic bombs, each threatening to blow up the others.

War takes a man's sons and daughters halfway round the world, and if they come back alive — and they were some of the lucky ones — they're no longer satisfied with home. Martha wasn't — and Reeder would never settle down, traveling all over the world as he had. And if young folk were content with their lives, there was the radio blaring away, telling them what was going on all over the world, stirring them up till they'd no desire to stay put.

But Willy was solid, he thought. He would manage all right. Still it was a pity he didn't take to farming. Reeder was Bessie's son, red head full of radio, television, nuclear fission — all kinds of information which Wilmont secretly thought had destroyed the world as he had known it. As for his daughters, if they had only been born twenty years earlier before all this free thinking, he might have been proud of them. Well, he had had his chance and failed. He sighed, helped himself from the platter and turned his attention to Davey.

Something about the child drew him just as he had been drawn to Gladine, the baby's mother — a frailty, an innocence that a man longs to protect, as though he could preserve it with his own strength. Foolishness, of course, an old man's foolishness. He'd spoiled Gladine with such notions, as Bessie had taken pains to tell him. That's the way it was with him — wanting to do the best for his children and doing the wrong thing every time.

Like enough he'd done the wrong thing making Gladine marry. He'd been so sure of himself, so sure he was right. Still what ought he to have done? A child couldn't grow up without a name — or could he? Nowadays he wasn't so sure about anything.

They fought, Gus and Gladine, scenes not right for a child to witness. Perhaps that accounted for Davey's being such a sober child and the wide wondering look in, his big brown eyes. Those eyes reminded Wilmont of the fawns he surprised in the woods among the ferns, all gangling legs and big soft eyes. Davey was tall for his age, but there was no meat on his bones.

Gladine spoiled him. She was passionately possessive of the one thing she had accomplished in life, Davey. She was wrapped up in him, thought she owned him, body and soul, never giving him the chance to be the individual the Lord intended.

"I don't aim to have any more children," she had told her Pa, "and I mean to keep him a baby just as long as I can." It wasn't right and he'd told her so. But she paid no heed, simply tossed her head and told him he'd brought up his family the way he wanted to and she aimed to bring hers up the way she wanted without any interference from him. He sighed deeply, remembering the little girl she had been and his own folly in not continuing to befriend her.

After dinner he'd take Davey to see the new piglets and when Britches had her kittens he'd give him his choice of the batch. Someday perhaps Davey would show an interest in farming. It was a real pity — all the effort he'd put into the place and no one to carry on when he was gone. But he knew it was only wishful thinking and sighed. What would the world be like when Davey was a man?

Emily Muir was born in Chicago in 1904 and came summers to Deer Isle as a child aboard coastal steamers. In 1939 she moved to Stonington with her husband, sculptor William Muir, where she began to paint, write and design houses. She's been there ever since. *Island Journal* (Vol IV, 1987) provides an in-depth profile of Emily Muir's prolific creative life.

Out There in the Dark

Alice Hildebrand Rudiger

It was blowing hard when they got up. Cathy twisted up her hair and went downstairs to start the coffee. Danny followed her, buttoning his woolen shirt as he came down the stairs.

"Jesus, I have a headache," he said ruefully, ruffling up his hair. "Guess I had too much last night."

"I guess you did," she said shortly.

"Mommy — Angie pooped," came the voice of Little Danny through the ceiling vent.

"I'll get them," Danny said.

Cathy started the kids' oatmeal and cut margarine into the pan for Danny's eggs. There were no sausages left. She mixed up juice, got out the milk, set the table.

Upstairs she could hear Danny talking like Yogi Bear while he changed Angie. "Hey hey hey, it's a great day!" he said. Little Danny could do it too. "Day!" said Angie.

They came into the kitchen on Danny's back, Angie crowing on the right shoulder, Little Danny on the left. He slid them off carefully into their chairs and sat down himself, reaching for the coffee pot.

"Day!" said Angie again, with a smile, and banged her spoon on the table.

Cathy fixed the oatmeal with milk, raisins and sugar and gave them each a bowl. She slid three eggs over easy and four pieces of toast onto Danny's plate. She poured herself a cup of coffee.

"So what did I say last night, anyway, then?" he said as she turned back to the counter and pulled out the sandwich makings for his lunch.

Little Danny squealed as he knocked over his glass of juice. Cathy caught the glass as it rolled for the floor and swiped at the spill with the dishcloth. A horn blew in the yard.

"Is that Seth already? Christ, I'm late," Danny said, shoving back his chair.

Seth came up onto the porch and grinned through the window.

"Come in and have a cup," said Cathy, opening the door to him.

"Well now, well now, sounds good, sounds just fine," said Seth. "Sounds just fine on a day like this one. That's a good wind out there. Yes sir!"

He took the coffee she held out, and with one hand pulled out his pack of Camels, maneuvered a cigarette into his mouth, put the pack away, got out his matches, and lit up. She put an ashtray near him on the counter and turned back to Danny's sandwiches — two baloney, one tuna fish, one cheese with peanut butter.

Seth leaned over to Little Danny and took off his cap. "Watch my ears, young feller, now watch 'em. You too, missy," he said to Angie. The children watched intently. His ears moved back and forth, back and forth, independently of each other. Little Danny screwed up his face and jerked his head from side to side. "Did I do it, Seth? Like that? Did my ears move? Did you see?" he asked.

"Well now, it takes a lot of practice, young feller. Now you watch this."

With her back turned, Cathy knew he'd be blowing smoke rings and doing something that looked like smoke was coming out of his ears. She'd never figured that one out.

"I saw your mother over to Gladys's yesterday, Cathy," said Seth, straightening up. "She said to tell you if you need anything she's going over to town Saturday with Vic and Tracy. Hey, here's the boy!"

Danny came into the room with his gear and took the lunch box she held out. Seth swung down over the table and growled like a bear. The kids shrieked in half-terror, half-joy. Danny searched her face for a minute, and she knew he saw what he was looking for. The lines around his eyes loosened up a bit; he leaned over and kissed her. Then he tumbled kisses onto the kids' heads and he was gone.

They heard the doors of the truck slam and the gears complain as Seth backed around in the dooryard. Seth's voice rang out over the noise " . . . got to haul them up today, blowing or not, hey boy," and he laughed.

The sun was coming in through the side windows now. Cathy lifted Angie out of the high chair and wiped her face, then turned the kids loose in the living room with their toys.

The cove was gray slashed with silver as clouds swept over and past the pale sun. There was one sailboat still moored out from the summer; its metal rigging chimed and slapped in the wind.

Danny's father and his father's father had moored their boats there. Old Pinky Leonard had lost his dock and his boat in the big winter storm of Danny's eleventh year, and there had never been money to rebuild the dock or buy another boat. Pinky had eked out a living as a stern man, done some clamming, cut some wood. He died of a heart attack when Danny was thirteen, dropped dead in his tracks picking up a half-full hod after years of hauling traps that weighed ten times more. Glady always said he'd died of a broken heart.

Cathy poured herself another cup of coffee and sat down in the kitchen rocker. She could see stripes of sun on the rug now, and the geraniums in the east window were aflame. As the sun pulled higher into the sky the gray and silver became robin's egg and cobalt blue. The wind was from the northwest and was not dying down any.

Last night Danny had drunk enough to start crying and to tell her she was killing him. She and Little Danny and Angie were killing him. He had put his head down on the kitchen table and wept. Cathy sighed and rubbed her forehead hard. Her eyes felt dry, so dry they wouldn't cry for a hundred years.

It was after eight o'clock. Eulie would be along soon to drop off her kids on her way to work. She took care of Mr. Pemberton, a wealthy old man from Philadelphia who stayed on the island from April until Christmas every year. It was a good job. Cathy had never been able to find more than just summer work for people from away. Eulie had probably been at the meeting last night too, with her husband Jack, who fished. Eulie was always in the thick of things. She'll be able to tell me what happened to get Danny so upset, thought Cathy.

"Mommy, come see Angie," called Little Danny from the other

room. Angie was jumping about in a little dance to the tune of her jack-in-the-box. Little Danny giggled with her, and Cathy smiled at them, their joy breaking through the weariness and confusion inside her. Angie tripped over her bear and sat down hard. Little Danny applauded, and after an uncertain moment, Angie clapped too. "Gre' day!" she said.

Eulie and her kids came into the kitchen on a rush of sound. Harold was five and would be with Cathy until nine o'clock, when Joan LePage picked him up for kindergarten. Mandy was the same age as Little Danny.

"It sure is blowing out there," said Eulie, shaking her curls back and lighting a cigarette.

"Coffee?"

Eulie glanced at the clock. "Real quick," she said.

"So what happened?"

"What happened?"

"At the Co-op meeting."

"Oh — not much. They just went around again about dragging and whether it hurts the clamming and what the marine biologist from the state said." Eulie took a big drink and drained her coffee, set the mug in the sink, and lit another cigarette. "Bye, Harold and Mandy. I'll see you at three-thirty. Be good!" she called. "Got to run, Cath. Maybe we can talk later." She was gone in a whirl of red, her jacket and scarf flying out behind her.

Cathy filled the sink with hot sudsy water and piled in all the dishes. Mandy and Angie came in to watch, so she put them at the table with play dough. She stood by the sink, watching the suds fluff up over the edge of the dishes, thinking.

Danny had wanted to be her boyfriend from grade school days. Even when they were teenagers and went to school on the mainland, everyone knew that Danny Leonard thought Cathy Jones was something special. But Cathy's father had not been impressed. "That whole family's mixed up. They've never been right since Pink lost the boat. That Danny'll never amount to anything," he'd growled at her often.

Cathy's brother Joe had been killed in Viet Nam just before her senior year in high school. That summer her father had sat at the kitchen table almost every night, crying with his head on his arms. He had three daughters left at home, but his son was gone. There was no son left to give the store to, no one to give the house to. There would be no new generation of Joseph Joneses living on Burnt Head Road. One night Cathy had come in late from a day of blueberrying with her friends. They had been to Sheep Island in Jack Hardy's boat, Eulie and Jack, Cathy and Danny, Amelia and Vaughn. She was sunburned and scratched, salty and hoarse, and happy from the holiday. She came quietly into the kitchen and saw her father sitting at the table, staring at his hands. He turned and looked at her standing there, barefoot in jeans and T-shirt and said, "Why couldn't God have taken you instead?"

She had run out of the kitchen into the starry August night, pelting barefoot down the dusty road after Danny, who had walked her home.

She had caught up with him out there in the dark and said, "Danny, I want to marry you!"

She had never told him about what her father had said that night. They married right after graduation and went to live in the big old house on Leonard Cove. Danny's mother had moved out to a trailer on the other side of the island. Danny had gotten a job with the state working on road projects.

Angie broke into her reverie, displaying a pink play dough chicken. Joan pulled into the yard in her old Chevy station wagon, and Cathy bundled Harold out the door, waving to Joan as she did so. Little Danny watched wistfully as the car drove away.

"Never mind, squirt, you'll go next year," she said to him, ruffling up his hair. With it standing on end he looked just like his father.

"Cathy, Cathy, look," called Mandy from the living room window. Flocks of eiders were landing on the water in sheets of black and white. Angie held up her play dough chicken and said, "Brock, brock?" Cathy laughed and hugged all the children for a moment, standing in the panels of warmth that came sliding through the windows, with the fiery red geraniums, and the black and white pattern of ducks falling like a blanket over the steel blue ocean.

She poured apple juice for all of them, got out the graham crackers, and went to do the upstairs work. Danny and she had the room Danny had been born in, in fact probably Leonards had always been born there up until Cathy's kid had come along. She and Danny had closed off most of the upstairs rooms. The house had been built long ago, when families ran to a dozen or more people.

Scooping up the laundry basket and the diaper pail, she headed down the narrow back stairs. It was hard on Danny that for seven years, the whole time they'd been married, he'd always worked in someone else's boat. It was hard on both of them that they lived in this big old house, moldering in its unused rooms, its boxes of family photographs, Pink's old waders in the basement, Danida's blue glassware in the pantry. The broken dock that had broken Pinky's heart could be seen from every window on the east side.

While she was in the basement, she shook up the fire and added more coal. They were getting low. Already! Winter hadn't even started yet. What was Danny going to do after he and Seth didn't go scalloping. Fewer of the men did now, after the burst of enthusiasm awhile back. She stood in the basement, rubbing her forehead, listening to the thumping of the kids in the kitchen, not seeing the familiar things that cluttered her life.

She started back up the stairs. There was nowhere she wanted to go, the island was their home. But it was harder and harder to live here. Her mother helped in whatever little ways she could without Dad knowing. And Cathy took whatever help she could without Danny knowing. They were all so proud. And I am too, she thought fiercely. But I can see things like Angie's sneakers getting too small. Like Little Danny needing to have his eyes checked soon because he squints all the time.

The long day of kids and housework passed slowly. In the late afternoon she watched the sun disappear into the thick black stand of spruce on the hill across the road. She waited for Danny. He came when the sun was gone, and the flamingo color was out of the sky. She heard Seth's old truck pull into the dooryard and idle there briefly. She opened the door into the thick cold blueness of the night settling in. Danny trudged across the yard, exhausted.

They sat at the table and ate corn chowder, hot dogs, biscuits Eulie had dropped off. Angie said, "Day, Dad-dad?" and Danny smiled at her. After supper he sat in the armchair by the window, and both kids climbed on him while she did the supper dishes. Angie brought him *Winnie the Pooh*, and he read to them.

It was the story about Eeyore losing his house and looking for it. Cathy felt a lump in her throat. Now that's ridiculous, she thought. I'm not losing my house. But somehow she felt like the donkey, wandering through the fields in search of his vanished home.

They took the kids upstairs together and tucked them in. Danny sat with Little Danny for a long time, the moonlight streaming in through the window. He murmured a quiet sleepy tale about all the nighttime things that were happening outside in the dark. Cathy kissed Angie good night and stood in the hall a moment, listening.

Danny came into the kitchen and sat at the table with her while she darned socks. He lit a cigarette.

"So — you want to tell me about last night, right?" he said to her.

"I want *you* to tell *me* about it," she said.

"Nothing to tell. The meeting didn't get anywhere, just gave people another chance to call each other assholes. Afterwards I went over to Benny's for a beer. I had a few, then I came home."

She looked at him a long minute. "Danny — last night you said me and the kids were killing you. You sat right here at this table and said we were killing you. You were crying." She kept her eyes right on his face.

His eyes were like Eeyore's.

"Oh, Danny," she said. She put down the socks and went around the table to him.

He drew her onto his lap. "Cathy — I wish I hadn't said that. I wish I'd never even thought it. I wish I didn't ever feel that way. You and the kids are all that I've got. Without you I'd be nothing. But if I hadn't married you I wouldn't be stuck on this island. I'd be gone from here."

She sat on his lap, stunned. "You mean you want to leave?"

"My life is such bullshit, Cath. Look at me — I'm nearly thirty, I can't pay my bills, now I've got nowhere to work for the winter again. Fishing's not what it used to be anyway. And we can hardly pay the taxes on this place. Look at my ma — living in a trailer on the dump road. Look at all the old folks — moving to Florida. Who're our neighbors — seven people from New York City whose names we don't know. I can't stand it here, but I can't leave because of you and the kids."

She leaped off of his knees. "You can go fuck yourself, Danny Leonard," she said. "You can go screw. Don't do us any favors. We can live without you. This island's my home, and it's where I *want* to be. You go look for someplace better."

He put his head in his hands. "There is no place better," he said. "That's why it's killing me. I don't want to leave either. But in Portsmouth or Gloucester I could stay busy enough not to think."

"Stay drunk enough, you mean." she shot back.

He sat just outside the yellow circle of the lamplight, his face and clothes were dark. She stood next to the table, with the light on her hair and clothes, regarding him defiantly.

"Cathy," he said, "Cathy, I don't know what to do."

She rubbed her forehead. "I don't either."

"I'm going up to bed," he said.

She nodded. He stood and kissed her. They held each other for a moment, loosely, politely, like relatives who rarely see each other, meeting at the side of somebody's grave. He turned and headed up the stairs. She watched his back ascend into the dark.

Then she reached up and turned off the lamp. The kitchen was instantly flooded with the silver of the moon. She walked to the windows that faced the water and stood looking out at the unquenchable night. It was still windy. The moon was so bright it masked the stars, and the choppy water gleamed like spangled fabric.

She thought of animals that loved the night, of all the lives continuing, hidden out there in the dark. The rafts of ducks afloat on the icy water at dawn. The living that goes on in secret, whether human eyes are there to see or not.

She turned back into the quiet house where moonlight picked out Angie's blocks and Little Danny's teddy bear. Around the room the darkened pictures of dead Leonards hung. She headed up the stairs after Danny.

He heard her undressing and said, "I'm awake." She slid into their bed naked, and he drew her into his arms. They slept, coiled together, while the cold wind blew off the Atlantic and swept around the edges of the house.

Alice Rudiger lives in Brooklin, Maine, with her seven-year-old son, James. She graduated from Bangor Theological Seminary in June, 1987, and is feeling her way towards some combination of ministry within the United Church of Christ, the islands of Maine, and writing. This summer she is a cook-apprentice at the Hurricane Island Outward Bound School.

Letters from
our Bay Correspondent

Unexpurgated for your Reading Enjoyment

Peter H. Spectre

Dear Editor:

E.H. Morgan and I closed the Iron Point Marine Antiques Exchange for the season and have embarked on a long-overdue sabbatical. We're spending the winter as caretakers at the lobster pound out on Crotch Island next to the Deer Isle Thorofare. We live on a barge moored next to the pound. I'm in charge of lobsters and E.H. is in charge of security. Once every two hours E.H. steps outside with his H&R over-and-under and fills the sky with lead. There isn't a poacher in Stonington across the Thorofare who doesn't get the message.

To fill up our spare time, Morgan plans to write his monograph on the history of the Fox Islands Carry Boat, which is what originally got us together more than ten years ago, and I'm going to explore the inlet at Crotch Island (the crotch of the island, so to speak) for more clues to the origin of the Sippewissett Marsh Boat, rumored to have been used as a granite lighter for the quarries.

Fred Brooks
Crotch Island, Maine

71

Dear Editor:

The strangest thing happened the other night. E.H. Morgan has been suffering from insomnia. He was rattling around for hours, talking to himself and poking through papers — "Where the hell are those canceled checks?" "That jughead Brooks has been reading my letters from Marylou." "Seed catalogs . . . seed catalogs . . . where the deuce are the seed catalogs?" About midnight I kicked him out and told him to row across the Thorofare to Stonington and see if he could find a drunk to roll or something if he had so much energy to spare.

About 3 a.m. I was awakened by a wild thrashing outside the cabin and weird gurgling sounds. I ran out and found Morgan beating the snow off the spruce trees with an oar and yelling about strange somethings that were out to get him. He turned on me and almost cut me in two with the oar, so I felled him with a piece of stovewood and dragged him to bed. That cured the insomnia.

E.H. came to the next morning with a lump on his skull and a horrible headache. At first he wouldn't tell me what happened. Then he said he was rowing back across the Thorofare and stopped to admire the winter stars while he pissed over the rail. A woman's hand came out of the water and grabbed the cuff of his trousers and pulled him over the side. He saved himself by grabbing the gunwale and kicking the hand free with his other foot. He's convinced the hand wasn't attached to a body.

When I went down to bail the boat that morning, there was a note tacked to the thwart with an icepick. It said, "Be smart. Don't count the lobsters and keep away from town." I didn't tell Morgan, but I'm beginning to wonder about the spruce trees myself. I'm also beginning to wonder whether keeping watch over poachers is the proper way to get away from it all.

Then things got worse and worse. The fish-house was broken into a couple of times when we were ashore getting supplies. Whoever it was left bizarre, threatening notes. Morgan swears they were putting something in our drinking water too. We got so paranoid we wired our resignations to the owners of the pound and hitched a ride on a Boston Fuel tanker to North Haven to reopen the Exchange.

Damn, it's great to be back in an honest business!

Fred Brooks, Prop.
Iron Point Marine Antiques Exchange
"Our Goods Are Your Goods"
North Haven, Maine

Dear Editor:

This summer has been fantastic for the marine antiques business! Even the general store has been going great guns. The town has been jumping. . . . More than that, it's been thrashing like a school of bluefish in a menhaden seine. People with ice cream cones are walking the streets and hanging around the pier and getting on and off the ferry boat. The local folk are cheating the summer folk and the summer folk are talking to God (or are they walking on the water? . . . no matter). We're selling antiques to all comers.

You ought to stop by before we're sold out. We have, of course, a full range of Taiwanese brass binnacles and diving helmets and a half-dozen or so plastic whalebone corsets, not to mention three or four properly "distressed" seaman's chests (we have a fellow out by the town dump taking care of those on contract), but we only sell that stuff to tourists. We do have some most genuine articles on hand for your inspection. (As you probably remember, we have three grades here in the Exchange — genuine, more genuine, and most genuine.) We have an old make-and-break engine, a more recent jump-spark model, a crate of flognarts (they need new hip-bottoms, however), half a dozen 12" engine telegraph repeaters, a very rare bobsprout from a 1927 Fay & Bowen speed launch, the main bower from a down east packet ship, a box of carbon copies of some rather erudite correspondence concerning nautical matters, and a most interesting shucklestay, said to have been hand forged in Copenhagen by O.L. Larsen, the greatest blacksmith ever to ply the trade.

Oh, yes, Morgan just brought in an extremely rare Seal Cove Eel Trap. This quite ingenious trap works on the diminishing-circle principle. It allows the eel to enter and then forces him to circle down through a tubular funnel. By the time the eel gets to the bottom his body is so tightly coiled he can't get out.

Fred Brooks, Prop.
Iron Point Marine Antiques Exchange
"Antiques Made to Order"
North Haven, Maine

Dear Editor:

We were ashore on Eagle Island the other evening and E.H. Morgan came across an old issue of *Motor Boat* magazine on the veranda of one of the cottages. I had just dropped a nice fat pheasant with my Whammo Wrist-Rocket. Deadly instrument. The bird's last grunt coincided with Morgan's groan.

At first I thought I had shot Morgan instead of the bird, especially since E.H. rolled over on the ground with the open magazine covering his face. But he was reading, not expiring — he's frightfully far-sighted. The groans were of pleasure, not pain. Morgan loves to read about fast boats.

By and by, Morgan plucked the pheasant and was roasting it on a spit. Or was he spitting on the roast? It was difficult to tell because it was getting dark. No matter. All of a sudden he started to sob and when I asked him what was the matter he began telling me about the summer of '28 and a strawberry blonde and the smell of honeydew melons and the lake in the moonlight and the perfume of her body (dear God!) and the leather of the upholstery and the roar of the engine and the slap of the water as it hit the bottom of the boat and the hope and the promise and. . . . Sweet Baby Jesus, we've lost our youth and will never get it back.

Fred Brooks, Prop.
Iron Point Marine Antiques Exchange
"The Least for the Most is the Best"
North Haven, Maine

Dear Editor:

We cured the late-winter heebie-jeebies with a boat race last week between Sid Waterman and E.H. Morgan in sprit-rigged peapods. The rules were simple — out to the red nun and back. It was a modified LeMans start. When the gun was fired, Sid and E.H. had to drink a pint of Old Overholt (chaser optional), then run down to their boats and go.

What a race! It was a straight tacking duel out to the nun, with Morgan singing "Shenandoah" so loud all the black ducks got up and left the harbor. As they rounded the mark, E.H. fouled Sid. Sid got mad and threw a boathook, missing Morgan but putting a big tear in his sail. E.H. got mad and hit Sid on the side of the head with a bailing bucket. They crossed the finish line neck and neck, screaming and hollering and heaving loose gear at each other. Sid demanded a rematch, while E.H., laughing like a lunatic, punched holes in the side of Sid's boat with a spare oar.

The judges ruled the race a draw and awarded the prize, a case of George Dickel's Sour Mash Whiskey, to the crowd. Locally the race has become known as the Dean Martin Classic and we intend to run it again next year.

Fred Brooks, Prop.
Iron Point Marine Antiques Exchange
"We Have What You Will"
North Haven, Maine

Dear Editor:

We launched the big skiff the other day. Hank O'Neal came on over from Pulpit Harbor, the first time in months. Morgan and him got in their cups, and come launching time they had just about forgot what we had gathered for. Hank was to give the christening speech, but he was confused and thought we were going to bury the boat.

It was a rousing oration — all about the glories of the boatbuilding wars and we'll never see the likes of these skiffs again and damn the United States Yacht Racing Union and it's a shame we have to bury this boat and why don't we at least burn her for her fastenings and does anyone in the crowd have a match and how about a little gasoline to soak down the garboards. . . . Before anyone could stop him, E.H. emptied a can of gas in the boat and Hank tossed a match into the thing. There was a Whump! and a pillar of flame and a lot of black smoke. Morgan was beside himself. He was weaving around the launching ramp egging Hank on: "Attaboy, Hank. We need those fastenings." By the time the Volunteer Fire Department put the flames out, the skiff was ruined. Marylou never even got a chance to christen the poor thing.

Fred Brooks, Prop.
Iron Point Marine Antiques Exchange
"Making Today's Antiques for Tomorrow"
North Haven, Maine

Dear Editor:

A fellow named T. Fremantle Fong stepped ashore from the ferry awhile back. He was dressed like an Englishman with a bowler hat, black umbrella, the works, and talked like Chiang Kai-Shek with a Lancashire accent. He said he was UPI's Far Eastern Correspondent. Morgan asked him why, if that was so, he wasn't in Hong Kong where he belonged. Fong said that North Haven was part of his territory "because it's far down east."

It seemed a trifle bizarre but logical enough, so we introduced Fong to all the right people as, in Morgan's words, a gesture of international friendship. Within days Fong took over the pool hall lease and turned it into a combination Chinese laundry and English tea room. I know you don't believe it, so I am enclosing a recent clipping from the *Island Record & Dispatch*:

Thorofare News

A supper will be held Monday to benefit the school nurse. Alvin Dickson is recuperating at the Togus Hospital and would like to hear from his many North Haven friends. The school lunch menu is posted at the town dock. T. Fremantle Fong has opened a laundry on the Back Island Road. The tick control officer will hold a clinic next Saturday in the town garage.

— *Alice Garland, correspondent*

There's more, much more. Fong started teaching a class in kung fu at the Odd Fellows Hall and an evening study group in Buddhism at the Southern Harbor Baptist Church. Then he took up a huge collection of money from the locals "for the poor starving children in China" and another "for the Cornish lifesaving service" and disappeared, leaving the laundry/tea room rent in arrears. E.H. is beside himself because he left his best clam-digging shirt in the laundry and now he can't get it back.

Fong is into us for more than the money he collected for the starving Chinese and the Cornish lifesaving service. He also has my custom-fitted alligator-hide clamdigger's gloves, the green ones with blue piping. I traded them to him for a set of shark's-teeth chess pieces in a nautical motif. It was a mistake. He got the genuine article. I got plaster of Paris. By the time I discovered I'd been had, that two-bit forked-tongued double-dealing snake-oil salesman from

Hong Kong had skipped town without even the courtesy of a "so-long-chump-you've-been-taken-to-the-(Chinese)-cleaners."

So far I haven't gotten back my Souvenir of Quebec clam-digging jacket (the silver lamé one), plus I've misplaced my designer mudflat boots. Keep your eyes open for them. Pink rubber, yellow Bill Blass signature, with a genuine Made in Malaysia stamp.

Fred Brooks, Prop.
Iron Point Marine Antiques Exchange
"Cheap Stuff Cheap"
North Haven, Maine

Dear Editor:

Strange doings over on the West Scrag. People from away were buying up property right and left, and some of the local boys were getting worried. So a special town meeting was called and an ordinance was passed that allowed the town to take vacant land by eminent domain. The wording said something about "collecting" these parcels of land for "the people's use." The opponents — which is to say, the people who hadn't yet had the opportunity to sell their land to speculators from New York — grabbed onto the terminology and started spreading the rumor that the local boys had turned Communist and were collectivizing the island.

Not long after that, Morgan and I were over to West Scrag on a field trip. We were down on the shore having a couple of beers when a Navy frogman crawled out of the water with a huge bolo knife and demanded to know if our lives were in danger.

"Danger?" Morgan asked. "What kind of danger?"

"You know," said the frogman. "From the collectivists."

And then all hell broke loose. There were parachutists and destroyers and strafing jet fighters and landing craft and who-knows-what-all. The frogman ran up the beach and captured the lobster-pound keeper and a helicopter landed on the beach and a couple of Marines hauled us inside.

"We're rescuing you from the Marxist-Leninists," said the lieutenant in charge, and before we knew it we were repatriated to Augusta. We never did get to finish our drinks.

Fred Brooks, Prop.
Iron Point Marine Antiques Exchange
"One Size Fits All"
North Haven, Maine

Dear Editor:

A fellow in a fancy suit came into the Exchange last week. He looked over all the wares, went out into the yard and poked around the building, came back in and looked out the window at the bay for awhile, and then said something like, "How much for everything?"

Well, I didn't know what to say. Did he want us to include the complete collection of left-handed sailmaker's needles? "Yes," he said. Even the box of rope ends and bent fishbox nails? "Yes," he said.

I was stumped. Nobody ever offered to buy all our stock at once. Morgan was in the back room reading seed catalogs, so I asked him what he thought we should charge.

"Does he want all the left-handed needles?"

"Yup."

"Does he want the rope ends and bent nails?"

"Yup."

"Well, I'll be damned. Tell him he can have it all for $800 and settle for $750.

So we made the deal at $745. The guy got all excited and wrote a check on the spot and Morgan and I got all excited and went into town and cashed it and got drunk.

The next day we were lying around the Exchange talking about some of the deals we had made. We were getting all choked up about the left-handed sailmaker's needles and running our hands through the bent fishbox nails when the guy stops by and asks when we'll be moving out, since he's going to convert the place to condominiums.

"When are we moving out?" I asked. "We were wondering when you were going to get your worthless shit out of our business establishment."

Then the awful truth set in. We thought we had sold him the stock only. He thought he had bought the entire property, the building, the land, the works. We showed the sales receipt to our lawyer. He says it's all legal and tight. We're out of business.

Fred Brooks

Peter Spectre of Camden, Maine, is a contributing editor of both *WoodenBoat* and *Down East* magazines. With the *Island Journal's* George Putz, he edited the seven-volume culturally uplifting *Mariner's Catalog*. He claims a proficiency in skipping stones, developed while waiting for something — anything — to happen when he lived on an island at the west end of the Cape Cod Canal as a boy.

Island
The Story of the Family Beal

Kathleen Snow

1524

Aguahega Island, "the landing place," didn't belong to them. For 5300 years they had belonged to Aguahega.

They called themselves Abnaki, "the people of the dawnland," for Aguahega was as far east as people could go. It was a mountain that had drowned, the island highest in a frigid blue bay, outermost. Its pink granite spine arched bare above forests of green. Lichens spun bullseyes of yellow across its 1,000-foot cliffs. In its mossy depths seventeen species of orchid hid, the shyest with a tiger-striped lip, lavender-pink petals, and three rows of golden hairs. At its root lobsters four feet long swarmed leopard-spotted blue, copper green, and orange — a surf of lobsters washing ashore after storms in heaps two feet high. Its mudflats spouted clams, its coves shrilled with seabirds: food to dry for the long mainland winters.

Beyond the ocean, to the east, only the sun had ever approached. But now something new rose there: a great canoe with three trees growing on it, trees with white clouds in their limbs. . . .

On the deck of *La Dauphine*, Verrazzano's carrack bristling with lombards that shot stone cannon balls, Girolamo the Mapmaker unrolled his 8½-foot parchment. Beneath the royal ensign of azure sprinkled with gold fleurs-de-lis, he sketched the landmark that was the high island, its twin claws of headlands spearing south into the sea. He named it Isabeau, the most beautiful of *le tre figlie di Navarra*, the three daughters of Navarre.

The island belonged to His Majesty Francois The First now.

1788

"How much *occopy* for the high island?" Amariah Beal called.

Amariah, his wife, Nabby, and their fourteen children were tired, grimy after sailing down east for eleven days from overcrowded Gloucester, looking for a cove, somewhere to settle, a home. And now, Amariah thought, they had found one. The high island was like a stronghold in which no harm could ever intrude.

"Worth very much." The Indian sagamore in his birchbark canoe squinted up at them from under a stovepipe hat. "Three gallons *occopy*."

Amariah looked his question at Nabby, heard her familiar mocking voice: " 'Take what you want,' said God, 'and pay for it.' "

Excitement bore him high and wild. Amariah rolled out three casks of their home-brewed cherry rum as the Red Man inked the exchange. "To Amariah Beal:

...a parcel of land commonly called by ye name of Aguahega, lying and being a Island in ye sea, bounded with Duck Isld on ye West, Burnt Isld and Barred Isld to ye East, Cape Andrews on ye north.
By the Hand of Joseph Quaduaquid, Sagamore.

1900

Gooden was the first of the Aguahega Beals to sell his birthright to someone from away. But tonight nothing could have been farther from his mind. His long square-tipped fingers reached for Mary Stella's waist, eyes shutting for an instant as the message of soft pink calico hot with the body beneath flashed through his palm, up his arm, racing into all the convolutions of his brain.

He had never held a girl's waist — other than a sister's — before. He always stood in the background braced by some wall, watching.

He opened his eyes: blinking through a sting of sweat. Mary Stella's pink and gold face danced before him, her blue eyes laughing up at him, her brown hair flouncing on the round white bertha collar that capped her shoulders, her black stockinged feet in the soft kip leather shoes flying to the music. He stumbled frantically to keep up.

On a box in the center of the room the bowlegged fiddler, suspenders dangling in scallops from his waist, leaned precariously forward as he sawed away at "Lady of the Lake." Beneath Gooden's heavy kag boots the rough planks bounced and thumped as they swept around with the others, finishing "Lady" and starting "March and Circle," down the long second-story packing room of the defunct lobster cannery. Through a haze of cigar smoke he glimpsed his father Perley and his mother in the crowds that lined the wall, and four of his seven sisters clapping their hands from their plank seats suspended between two kegs. Evelina, the youngest, crammed sticky brown dates in her mouth, spitting the stones back out on the floor.

Despite the thrown-open windows the heat was fierce, the reek of sweat heavy on the fog-dense night air. Mary Stella's face was red, glossed with moisture; but on her, even sweat looked good.

She was an angel, Mary Stella. She was *his* angel, should he go thinking of a bride some time soon, his mother kept hinting. For Gooden's eighteenth birthday Perley had given him 100 acres of his own to build a home on. He could clear the field for six cows, a yoke of oxen, fifty sheep, a couple of hogs. Mary Stella could tend the poultry while he fished, and every night they would go to sleep in each other's arms.

Because everyone knew Mary Stella was his.

Behind the cover of spinning her around he gave her waist a tiny experimental squeeze, his blood pounding when, coy as a herring at the mouth of a weir, smooth as a smelt, she sideslipped in his grasp, smiling wider up at him. Did she like him? Or was she laughing up at him — skinny-stick Gooden with his too-big ears jutting out in front of lank brown hair.

"Oo, Gooden, stop, stop!"

His heart stopped in panic, his hand dropping from her waist.

"We've just got to rest, can't catch my breath." She splayed her small pink fingers out against her collarbone. "I'd just love some of that nice cool lemonade before it's all gone."

"You wait just a second, Mary Stella. Fetch you a mug right back." He ran to the blue-painted wooden pail, dipping up two mugs and spilling it as he whirled, eyes scarching in confusion the spot where she had just stood.

It was the "Virginia Reel," the fiddler was tapping his toe, and Mary Stella was whirling down the floor in the arms of the young new preacher. *Angel? Angel?* Mary Stella simpered, eyes narrowed up at the preacher, looking at him from under her brows. The Devil take her, she was the Devil's own!

The tune was no more than finished when the preacher waved a halt. "Friends, I have a happy announcement. Mary Stella here's kindly agreed to become my wife."

Through the cheers Gooden heard only: "Got a powerful big thirst of a sudden, have you?" Harry Smallidge was mockingly eyeing the two mugs.

Gooden jerked away, the lemonade penetrating the front of his woolen pants, clawing down his legs in fiery cold lines. His family was looking, children laughing. He stood in a gray mist ringed with sound.

He fought his way down the narrow stairs, past the men stumbling up from the store below where they had fortified themselves with Ernie Taggett's keg of rum sweetened with molasses. He fled down the rutted cart path.

The night air was blessedly cool on Gooden's cheeks, hiding him in tattered islands of fog. It had been the longest fog mull on record, driving the mackerel schooners, with the fiddling sailor aboard, and a ship from foreign parts into the Aguahega village harbor. The Thoroughfare was a forest of masts: schooners, lobster smacks, and even the floating junkshop of a trader in whose shingled clapboarded miniature of a house on decktop Gooden had swapped clams, ten cents a quart, for the new doll buggy for Evelina, his favorite sister.

Faintly now, for the second time this evening he heard a violin, but this one's voice was slow and tremulous. Gooden felt its sadness merge with his own. It was coming from the other world of Aguahega, the summer world of Seal Point, where the rich had built Tenhaven, the first of the great shingled estates. In his torment he followed the music, avoiding Seal Point's ornamental iron gates, its boardwalks — strung like beads with pagoda-roofed gazebos — that rollercoastered over the hills. He walked through the silent wet skirts of evergreens to Tenhaven's garden wall, mauve with flowers, and peered through its round Moon Gate.

Colored lanterns smudged and winked blue, green, lemon from every tree. They ringed the fountain in the middle of a greensward whose flower colors faded into mist. People sat in wicker chairs and crowded in groups and the violin's playing, the most beautiful sound Gooden had ever heard, swelled from somewhere in their midst.

He stepped closer, hiding behind a stone pedestal ringed with frogs, on which stood a statue of a naked boy, stone blind. It was the girl he stared at, and he felt suddenly angry despite his fascination, because she made him realize Mary Stella wasn't beautiful after all. The girl's back was arched against some sort of tension, the blue glimmer of a paper lantern flickering over her blond hair. She wore a long gown of pleated white lawn and a man's hand like a decoration around her waist, hidden out here at the edge of the crowd. The man's fingers were beginning a slow, arduous ascent up the sheer face of her ribs. Higher they climbed, pioneering their way pitch by pitch, one, two, three fingers gaining altitude, regrouping, now setting forth boldly again, higher, higher, closing inexorably toward the overhang of her breast.

Gooden felt as if the blood would burst from his ears.

Underbrush crackled behind him.

Every pore of Gooden's body burst open, pouring sweat as the man's fingers ascended the first foothill of the final peak.

The underbrush in the woods behind him snapped alive. A boyish voice hissed out at him, and then another, and another.

"Edward, do you *notice* something?"

"Why, no — oh, could you possibly mean that sudden stink?"

"Old fishermen don't die. They just smell that way."

"Why'nt they take a bath?"

"They haven't got a bath!"

"Turpentine wouldn't get that off. That's fish stink. They all stink, all the natives do. Tell them coming a mile away."

"Reek, rank, runk,
all the fishermen stunk.
Runk, rank, reek,
their mothers also stink!"

There were seven of them in their mid-teens, and though he was half a head taller than the tallest of them, they were strangely awesome, these children of the rich.

He was trespassing, and he backed away through the Moon Gate into a maze of boxwood and Blackthorn hedges.

"You were *spying*, weren't you?" He was the biggest of them, redhaired with white eyelashes, in knickerbocker pants and knee socks. His stiff finger jabbed Gooden's chest.

"No."

"Come here to steal, you stinking sneak thief?"

Gooden turned around but there was one of them behind him, short with slitted narrow eyes. Gooden pushed through a narrow arched opening in the hedge. Ahead was another wall of yellow stucco, again with a round doorway and Gooden ran through. But inside was enclosed without exit, a graveyard with miniature headstones and urns sculptured of privet with roses.

"I meant no harm."

"Planning to steal, huh, sneak thief? Just pop right in and pinch a few things?"

"He stinks worse'n a garbage pit."

Shame pushed Gooden harder than their jabs and shoves, rode him as closely, as indelibly as his smell. He had discovered it the first time he ventured inside one of the great "cottages," delivering a package from the post office to earn some change. The endless front hall was white and gold, fragrant with waxed wood, sunlight gleaming on the polished floor and carved walls, shining through the window in a room at the end of the hall, the biggest window he had ever seen.

The woman's straight small nose had wrinkled as he stood there, she in her black uniform with an apron lacy as a doily, and it was then he was first aware he had a smell.

The smell. But then they all had it, all of the fishermen — the fish smell that clung to clothes, penetrated the skin, breathed out of your pores no matter how hard you scrubbed. "It smells like money," his mother said. "You hesh up and don't go giving yourself airs."

Now, at Tenhaven, Gooden watched the short boy wrap a handkerchief around and around his knuckles. He flexed his fingers, making a fist. "If I saw a snake coming at me and a native, I'd let the snake go free."

"Let him go!" The boy was younger than the rest, ears that jutted like handles on a jug, tweed kneepants and matching tweed cap. "Charles, it's my property. I say let him go."

"Shut up, Fairfield!" The tall redhead spared him no glance. "You're just chicken. How about you, Edward? What do you say?"

A fist spun out of the air, colliding with Gooden's chin. The darkness in his head exploded into light. He felt his thighs bunching, he was sailing through the air and his own fist connected with someone's hard bone. But abruptly he felt his arms pinned back, four of them twisted his arms higher, higher until he fought to keep from shrieking with pain. The redhead and the short one approached him from the front. He stared like a deer shined by gunners: it knew it was going to get it, transfixed.

When the beating was done Gooden found himself flat on his back. Moisture soaked up into his shirt. Or was it blood, soaking down into the ground? He struggled to breathe. There was a shivering deep inside him, as if his intestines had come loose.

"Oh, Charles," one of them said, falsetto. "Whatever are you doing now?"

Gooden felt the urine land spattering on his pants leg, hot as it soaked through the sieve of cloth. The sound of the last few drops ratcheted through his brain. He tried to get up but his legs didn't work, his brain swam through a new endless sound. It was a sound like rain falling. It fell on his knees, his stomach, his chest, it sluiced his face. His body steamed with it, vapor rising in the night like artic smoke.

When they had been gone awhile Gooden dragged himself to his knees. The spruces spun and blurred. And then he saw the youngest one again.

Fairfield Chancellor was staring at him as if he were a strange marine creature washed ashore. His voice piped high: "I tried to stop them. I'm sorry." A new dollar bill fluttered in his outstretched hand. "Can you get up?"

The pity Gooden saw in his face was the worst shame. It brought him roaring to his feet. The tweed kneepants vanished through the round doorway in the wall.

Gooden rolled in the clipped clean grass, dragged his wet arms and legs over it and through it, pulled it up, crushing it, rolling it over his face. His face was wet with the green juices and his own tears. He ran stumbling through the woods, afraid to take the road, following the ridge trail down the backbone of Aguahega to Alewife Pond. Without removing his clothes he jumped in, swimming through the icy purity of white lily pads, splashing deeper in his clumsy dogpaddle until the numbing cold sank too deeply into his blood. He came out pouring wet and stood trembling on the hill above Perley's house.

But he couldn't go in. Gooden stared down at his home.

He smelled the smell of urine even in his hair.

He knew it would never wash clean.

· · · · ·

"Reek, rank, runk,
all the fishermen stunk.
Runk, rank, reek,
their mothers also stink."

Gooden closed his eyes and let the train take him westward, deep into the main. The black rampart of Aguahega was far away, fog covering it like a shroud. But the voices of the rich boys pursued him, faster than the train, louder than its wheels.

He lay on top of the freight car watching the fleece of unfamiliar clouds unroll over his head. He had $200 in his pocket; it was unbelievable but there it was. He remembered the chalked message on the schoolhouse blackboard: "Seest thou a man diligent in his business? He shall stand before kings; he shall not stand before mean men." He would be diligent in his business, Gooden decided, see the world, make a fortune as large as any at Seal Point. And the money in his pocket was the match that would start the flame. . . .

Again he drew out the folded document, squinting in the sun as he read the incomprehensible words.

This indenture made the thirteenth day of the eighth month in the year of our Lord nineteen hundred.

Between Gooden Henry Beal, herein designated as the party of the first part and Altoona Land Company, herein designated as party of the second part.

Witnesseth, that the party of the first part granted, bargained, sold, aliened, enfeoffed, released, conveyed, and confirmed unto the said party of the second part, heirs and assigns, ALL that tract and parcel of land. . . .

It sounded like the Bible but it didn't mean a thing. He could feel the land in him indelible as a birthmark, as deep as sin. You could never wash it away.

By nightfall there were four travelers preparing for uneasy sleep in the depths of the "side-door pullman": the rattling boxcar. The red-haired woman lay down beside Gooden, her dark eyes with the deep circles searching his, and spread her one thin blanket over them both. Under the blanket he felt her fingers fumbling, tugging at the buttons on the front of his wool pants.

In the blackness she pulled him suddenly on top of her, her bare thighs breaking around him like water, like waves. He looked down into the denser blackness where her face should have been. It seemed he was looking at Mary Stella's face, pink and gold and then snuffed out, like a candle flame between finger and thumb.

When he woke in the morning the woman and the $200 were gone.

Kathleen Snow has published a novel, *Night Waking* (Simon & Schuster), and an article, "My Liberated Mind Has A Wuthering Heights Heart," in *Harper's Magazine*. "Island: The Story of the Family Beal" is an excerpt from a novel of the same name, and is based on true tales of the Snow family history. Snow has dropped her "killick" in New York City.

The Turnip Yard

Peter Scott

O n the first day of the season Oscar Gross went down to the cove early. He limped like an old pirate, favoring the leg that had stiffened in the night. It was a clear, chilly dawn, the first week in April. The tide was all the way gone, as low as it ever gets, and far out at sea on the horizon was a thin line of haze scaling north toward Nova Scotia. Overhead a solitary cloud, barely the size of a man's hand, lingered inside the land. There was a light breeze baffling in and out of the cove, and his boat, which he and George had piled high with traps the night before, tipped precariously from side to side on her mooring.

When George arrived, still half asleep as usual, they said something about the weather, then set to work loading the ballast stones heaped at their feet. Oscar went below and waded through the muck to bring in the skiff and secure it to one of the pilings. George watched sleepily from the wharf, his hands snuggled inside his sweatshirt, until he was aroused by an unhappy voice from below:

"Don't hurry on account of me," came the voice. "I've been looking forward all winter to standing in cold water up to my ass."

George moved reluctantly to the edge, not bothering to hide the smile in the corner of his mouth. From the height his friend looked small and crumpled.

"All right, all right," he said wearily. "How should we do this?"

Oscar sighed, impatient. "The same way we did it last year, and the time before that. What'd you think? Drop them here away from these other rocks so they won't break, and I'll load the skiff." He paused. "Or maybe you better aim *for* the rocks — then you can be sure you won't hit them."

George began to drop the heavy stones over the edge, two at a time. Within minutes they had established a rhythm: two stones falling as Oscar loaded two. George dropping as Oscar turned aside. The work warmed them, and they both welcomed the familiar confidence that grew as they leaned and rose in perfect time, without wasted motion.

Oscar grumbled as he sloshed back and forth between the skiff and the wharf. It was impossible to hear him clearly from above, but George knew what he was saying by pieces of sentences that rose from the water below. From simple habit he responded with a grunt of agreement every minute or so. He was quietly pleased to hear the complaining, as it meant they were at work again. He once told his sister that the two of them worked to the cadence of Oscar's grumbling like galley slaves worked to the beat of the drum.

But this time Oscar broke stride. He stopped on the shore and stood with his legs apart in the mud, and with one bent finger aloft toward the wharf, he scolded: "You can blame it on these new fellas — that come down here from Rockland in boats owned by some bank. They put out six hundred traps, half of them pairs, and then they turn around and wonder why there aren't any more lobsters. They. . . ."

"It's a good thing I looked over first." George stood at the edge with a big flat stone arrested in mid-swing. "I almost dropped this on your damned head. Maybe I should have. Maybe I should just keep dropping them on your head until I drive you into the mud like some clam. Then I couldn't hear your grouching."

"We don't need any more rocks, you fool. The skiff's loaded. If you'd look at what you're doing, you'd know that much. What do you think I'm standing here for?"

"Here, then, here's one more." He placed the last stone perfectly: it plopped flat in the mire at the old man's feet, making a sucking noise like a boot being pulled free from slime and splattering Oscar from his boots to his new cap with blobs of rank bottom mud.

"Oh, Jesus, Oscar!" cried George swinging a guilty fist, "I am sorry!" But he couldn't hold the laughter in, and went down with it, on his hands and knees, watching over the edge, laughing and apologizing at once.

Oscar stood without breathing, his hands held limp and spread away from his body as if avoiding contamination. A piece of glop loosened and dropped from his shirt as he stared at his front in speechless surprise. When he did look up, his arms still held outward, he had to blink to focus through the brown spots on his glasses, and shout to be heard above George.

"You goddamned jerk!" he finally managed. "You son of a bitch!"

But George swore it was an accident.

"Oh sure," said Oscar sputtering. "I ought to make you clean this shirt, or give it to your sister to do, you damn prune." He looked once more down to his clothes, then up again, releasing a round exhale of disgust that sounded like a blowing whale and almost rolled the laughing partner off the wharf.

When George settled down, they brought the boat out of the cove and turned south toward Oscar's fishing grounds. George sat on an upturned trap while Oscar stood quietly at the wheel dipping a fishy rag into a bucket at his feet and wiping fussily at his shirt. "You could at least have waited until I had my apron on, you clumsy bastard."

Oscar's fishing grounds lay a mile off the island on which he had been born. He had inherited the area through his great-grandfather who had claimed it years and years ago. It was a small area, running north to south on the weather side of the island, about three miles long and one wide. His fishing grounds included a place called the Turnip Yard: a deep bowl-shaped sea area whose eastern boundary is marked by a pair of bald islands called the Two Horsemen. At its southern end, the Turnip Yard is exposed to open sea. It has always been a coveted fishing area because of the ledges and rocky bottom so loved by lobsters, but even though they often wished aloud that they could fish there too, none of the other island fishermen ever asked because only Oscar knew the dangerous and unpredictable grounds well enough to fish them successfully, without loss of equipment in the ledges and queer currents.

He didn't need a depth recorder because he knew the bottom in his own area as well as he knew the warps in his kitchen floor. He had fished the Turnip Yard one way or another since he was fifteen, so it was no wonder he knew it like he did. First he fished it with his father, hauling traps by hand in an old one-lunger, then with Dunreath, his uncle, in Dunreath's boat; then he fished alone until he took on George twelve years ago. He had hated fishing alone because of the things that can happen to a man alone out there on the water, so, although he was skeptical of George at first, he took him on to have company, and it had worked out well enough.

Before George, Oscar had never had a close friend, unless you counted his Uncle Dunreath, who'd been dead twenty years. Dunreath was old enough to be his father when Oscar fished with him, and people on the island used to joke about them, the way they went around together all the time, an old man and a boy. Dunreath was too shut-mouthed and suspicious to have any friends left alive, and Oscar at thirty was already a grouch and some said a prude. Now they joked about him and George for the same reasons, and though he acted like he wasn't paying attention to what they said, Oscar was secretly pleased to have people put them together and talk about them like that. At first he thought George was over-confident when they were aboard the boat: he thought he took too many foolish chances. But after a few years some of that confidence began to influence even Oscar, so that he worried less when he was out on the water, and didn't hate it so much. Still, he wished George would be more careful when they were out on the water.

They worked most of the morning in the Turnip Yard in a growing sea. Oscar said there was probably a good-sized squall out to the southwest where the haze ended in clouds, and it would be the squall that was sending the low, rocking swells in toward them. George paid no attention, but continued to work among the traps and tangle at his feet, walking uphill and downhill on the deck, pausing occasionally to sprinkle a handful of salt onto the slippery boards beneath him.

When they had finished putting out the first string of traps, Oscar turned the bow into the gathering sea, and George came forward to stand under the house and pour a cup of coffee from his thermos. He braced himself against the side and unpacked the fresh doughnuts his sister had sent with him. Oscar held the wheel to his chest with his forearm, and unwrapped a thick sandwich with his free hand. He said something to George through the chewing mush.

"If you had your head underwater, it would be easier to understand you," said George in exaggerated disgust. "Didn't your mother ever teach you not to talk with your mouth full?"

Oscar swallowed angrily: "I said I can hardly get my food down, you stink of bait so."

"If you chewed it instead of talking into it, you might have a better chance. Besides," George added, looking into his tilting coffee, "it isn't me that stinks, it's that nasty bottom mud all over you that makes it hard to eat."

"And whose fault is that, you son of a bitch! This shirt was clean when I started out this morning." He took another mouthful of sandwich and swallowed it with a gulp of tea. While they talked the wind nosed the boat broadside into the swells and one low wave slapped against the side, spraying Oscar and his raised sandwich. George chuckled saying they ought to let her float against the swells a while longer: then maybe he wouldn't have to worry about washing any shirt when he got home.

"I don't like the looks of it," Oscar said after watching the sea. "One of those swells could turn us right over if it hit us right, with the boat loaded the way it is. The tide's still coming; it'll be high in an hour. It's going to get rougher before we're done."

George hated the thought of going back in, of failing to finish the first day out. He had been waiting for the old man to worry about the waves, and had prepared an argument.

"We've fished in weather worse than this," he said reasonably. "There isn't any wind to speak of."

"We never fished in this kind of water with the stern tipsy from traps piled up, and the whole damn boat canted to starboard with a load of stones."

"Maybe it will get too rough in an hour, but by then we'll have most of the traps overboard and half the rocks with them, unless we have to sit here and listen to you worry all morning."

To show that he meant it, George flung the rest of his coffee overboard and stuffed his mouth full of doughnut.

"All right," said Oscar, "but I tell you I don't like it. I've seen storms like this that could send in swells twice the size of a boat."

George bent to roll up his boots and stood behind, holding onto the low roof. The swells, running in from the open sea in irregular groups, were deep and well spaced, but they weren't cresting and didn't seem to be getting any bigger. As he turned, Oscar warned him to keep an eye on the top row of traps.

"You let me worry about the traps. You just watch those swells and hold us into them while I'm setting one. You wouldn't worry so if you knew how to swim."

"When are you going to understand that knowing how to swim doesn't make any difference?" Oscar shook his head at a history of stupidity.

"If I fell overboard," George said, "all I'd have to do was tread water until you came back around for me; or I could swim to the boat and get back aboard. Even if she was turned over, I could hang on, or maybe swim ashore."

"Sure," said the old man sarcastically. "You could hang on until you froze to death or drifted in and got squashed and smashed to bits on the rocks. A lot of good swimming would do you then."

"I wouldn't freeze to death because I'd keep moving. At least I'd have a chance: you'd never get back to the boat. You'd probably faint dead before you hit the water anyway, out of fear of it."

Oscar wanted to put the second string of traps in deeper water, but to stay out of the swells he headed closer to the lee of a long protruding ledge inside the Turnip Yard. George pointed to another fisherman farther out: "It doesn't look like he's spilling traps and equipment overboard, or breaking up on the rocks. It doesn't look like *he's* having any trouble at all."

"He doesn't have a talking monkey climbing all over his stern deck," said Oscar.

He took the boat in as close to the ledge as he dared, and George pushed the traps over into deep water at its foot. On the windward side of the ledge the swells, which had increased in size and regularity, were pounding against the rocks but making huge sullen thumping sounds as they slid into the rock wall and flattened against it. George thought the pushing swells sounded like snow sliding off a roof and landing in a quiet pile; Oscar thought they sounded like heavy swells striking a ledge, and he didn't like it one bit.

They came out from behind the ledge and into open water again. It was all the old man could do to hold the bow into the rising sea, and he almost got sick each time they heaved over one swell and slid helplessly down into the valley between it and the next. He swore and held the wheel, shouting over his shoulder that this was the last goddamned trap, he was going in while he had the chance. George told him to stop griping and watch what he was doing; he said it'd calm down some in a few minutes, there were only six traps left anyway.

If Oscar hadn't turned around to look nervously at George, he might have seen the solitary, monstrous swell that rolled toward his port bow. It came on alone, as if several swells had grouped and were seeking the shore in a single swollen mass that strained to keep from cresting before it struck. Before he could shout or even turn into it, the old boat rose broadside to meet it, drifting up the wall of moving water until the deck was almost vertical. The traps went first, tumbling off the stern, then George slid down the deck grabbing for something to hold before he went over backwards, followed by an avalanche of stones. Oscar managed to hold on for another second until he too dropped off and fell into the trough below. He struck the surface and sank, his body limp with surrender, and would have let out his breath and gone down with the familiar gear that drifted past him had he not seen George five yards away under water, a vague shape in the murky plankton, and thought that George could see him too as they danced there in the shifting green light. As he watched, George rolled over and began to climb toward the air, but he was struck by a sinking trap and pushed it aside only to meet the rest of the ballast stones that fell down on him like a slow rain of boulders, bumping his back and head. He flailed at the rocks, trying to climb at the same time, but one then another struck him in the face and he rolled once, released a cloud of bubbles, and began to sink with the stones, following them down in a slow fall.

Oscar did not look down, but thrashed toward the dark keel above. He broke surface at the stern and reached for the splashboard where he took hold and breathed through a rounded mouth, his legs tucked up underneath him. He must have taken the boat out of gear before he went over, though he couldn't remember doing it. Before he could get his breath back, the cold and the shock came over him at once, and he had to rest his chin on the splashboard to gather strength. With a terrible effort he hauled himself up over the stern and slid on to the deck where he lay wet and sucking for air with his eyes shut. If only he could lie there safe and wait until George, who must have been joking somehow, came up alongside and made remarks about him looking like a codfish just landed.

When he lifted himself dripping to his feet he saw that the boat was yet two hundred yards from shore and hardly drifting at all. The surface was almost calm, as if the giant wave had rolled it flat as it passed over in its run for the shore. He stood and squinted, trying to see without his glasses. Only one buoy had come up (it was bright red) and he could tell the other shape was the wooden bait barrel the way it rolled and ducked. "George!" he cried. "George!" At first his voice was cautious and questioning, for fear he had been tricked, but as he called out his cries became strained and angry, and he screamed his friend's name at the quiet surface.

He set the boat in gear and started in a slow hopeless circle around the floating tangle of rope and debris. After two luckless turns through the area, he took the CB mike and fumbled for a channel with voices.

The first boat came alongside in ten minutes. It was Jerden Hutchinson and his tall son. Jerden wanted him to come aboard his boat, and get a change of clothes, but Oscar didn't answer, so Jerden stepped over bringing dry clothes with him. At a signal from his father, the boy took the other boat and started in a larger circle, talking excitedly into the CB as he turned out. Jerden had the sense not to speak: he stood holding the clothes until Oscar changed his shirt, wrapped up in a blanket, and took a cup of whiskey colored by Coca Cola. As if there was hope, Jerden took the wheel and started her out in another circle behind his son. Oscar stood in the middle of the deck, almost hidden beneath the blanket over his head and shoulders. He held the cup in two hands before him and kept his motionless face toward the water.

Within a half hour, four other boats had joined them. Before each one started the search, it came alongside so the men could show that they had come. No one hailed Oscar or asked him any questions: they sailed by him with their faces set to match his, then turned outward into the search without a word. The younger men rode high on the bows of their boats, legs spread for balance and gaffs held ready before them. Though they knew before they came that they could find nothing and could say nothing, they continued in their slow circling ritual until early evening when they began to peel off one at a time, sliding by Oscar's boat and shaking their heads "No" once before they left.

When he got home he found a note from his wife leaning against the sugar bowl on the kitchen table. She said, as he had hoped she would, that she had gone to sit with George's sister. He changed his clothes and made some coffee and a sandwich and carried them into the back room, turning out any lights that might be seen from the road. He lay back on the sofa with his coffee balanced in his lap and shut his eyes.

It would be more than twenty-four hours before he floated to the surface, if he came up at all. The others would look for him to wash up on shore during the day, carried in by the tide. What they didn't know was that the tide, when it was going out, struck the point of land south of where he went down, so it curled and turned, and would carry him right back into the Turnip Yard. What they had in mind too was to bring George in and present him to his sister so she could bury him. As if they didn't know that the crabs would already be working on him, eating out his eyes and feasting on his fingers. What would that be like for her, or for anyone who knew George and how he could laugh at himself and encourage others to do the same? And the damned Coast Guard would be in on it too, young fools driving around on the water all night like George was just another carcass to be hauled out and bagged and numbered.

No, it was up to him to do it. He'd have to find him before he washed ashore and see to it that she'd never have to look at a ghoul for a brother, and maybe remember him that way. It would want luck to have him float to the surface at the right time, rather than stay under and come ashore that much later and that much worse to look at. When Dunreath's father drowned, they had to burn the crabs off him to keep from pulling away the soft flesh. The sight of him drove his wife half mad, as if she ever needed an excuse.

That night he listened to his wife console him, and answered her questions. He took a drink before he went to bed, but could not lie still in the room, so went back downstairs where he paced and napped half awake until mid-morning. During the day she kept visitors at the door, though she disagreed. That evening she went to see George's sister, saying as she left that she hoped he'd come too.

The tide was coming when he went down to the wharf in the dark. He had a gaff and a flashlight, and a full thermos. He loaded several of the flattest stones in the bow of the skiff, and slowly, not to get ahead of the tide, rowed out of the dark cove on his knees as if going out to the boat for yet another day of fishing. There was a light chop on the water, and a southerly breeze, but when he turned and sat down to row against it, he found little resistance, and staying close to shore, he headed down toward the Turnip Yard, watching now and again over his shoulder for the first signs of the moon. After a half hour of rowing he could make out the Two Horsemen waiting on the thin horizon. Using them as markers, he turned out into deeper water and slowed to watch the surface. The moon came up, its light diffused over the water, but it was little help because it was still low in the sky and the slanting silver caused a deceptive pocket of darkness under each little wave.

When he felt sure the tide was beginning to go out, he turned the skiff into the middle of the Turnip Yard and rowed against the wind toward the open sea. At the southern end he stopped rowing and let the wind carry him back. He knelt on the seat and watched over the stern, straining to see something he could not dare to imagine, assured only that he would know it if he saw it. But what if he bumped it in the dark? The little white-capped waves, the only sign of life all around, slapped at his stern, soaking him with a cold spray that stiffened his fingers on the oars.

Before he had made three passes over the Turnip Yard, the moon was high and he felt as though he'd been out on the water all night. If he missed George this time, he would miss him altogether, and he began to hope in spite of himself that he *would* miss him, and not have to see him this way: his face wet and swollen in that awful grey light, the eyes emptied by what they had already seen. If he had to say, he'd allow that the looking for him had been worse than watching him drown; at least under water it had happened and was done; here it was all waiting and the growing fear of what he'd come to find.

On the next pass he fanned the surface timidly with his light. He hadn't drifted a hundred yards when his beam passed over a dark rounded shape bobbing among the little waves. He must have passed him twice in the darkness. He knelt and watched, colder now and surprised at his own reluctance to move, as George's head drifted away from him. He brought the skiff around and circled the shape, shouting at it: "George! George!" until he could delay no longer and backed in toward it.

He was floating standing up, as if still climbing, or else walking in to shore on legs the length of shadows. Oscar came in behind him and tied one end of the line to the stern, looping the other end and letting it sink down over George's shoulders. He averted his eyes lest George turn and show him his face. When he had secured him, he sat down to row out toward open water. Once he slipped and looked against his will: he saw George's shoulders break the surface when he pulled on the oars, and his ears bend back when he sank again. "Almost," he said to encourage. "We're almost there." He had towed things before, a skiff with two men in it, but never anything this heavy, never anything that pulled against him like this.

He stopped when he was in the way of the outgoing current. From here he'd be carried out beyond the bay, and well into open sea before the tide turned and started coming again; by then he'd be wedged on the bottom, or taken so far out it would be New Hampshire before he washed up on shore. With his teeth clamped shut, Oscar reached over his friend with the gaff and carefully lifted the line free of his shoulders. At first he thought to drop the rocks down the back of his shirt so he wouldn't have to turn his face around, but that might roll him belly up, eyes to the moon, so he reached gingerly around to his throat and slid the first ballast stone down into his undershirt. George's head tucked forward, as if looking beneath him to see where he'd settle.

He slipped three of the biggest stones into his shirt all at once, and George hesitated, then sank effortlessly like another weighted trap. Oscar rowed off a few yards to sit and watch in case he came back up. He stood up in the skiff, sculling to hold his place, and studied the surface of the water, mumbling at first, then talking aloud, angrily: "It's all right for you now, George Weed. You're not the one who has to go out alone tomorrow, and every day after that. I'm the one who has to start fishing alone all over again."

He rowed for a mile without looking around, then when he got inside the land, he centered his stern on the tip of the second Horseman, and started back in toward the cove. She'd be the only one he'd tell, and even she wouldn't understand. She'd fault him for not giving George's sister the chance to bury him and pay her respects. She'd never understand that George would have expected him to do it the way he did: like it was just more damn work, only this time far lonelier than it had ever been before.

Peter Scott lives in Ohio and spends summers on Isle au Haut where he writes short stories, several of which have been published in small literary magazines. He is currently at work on a novel which he describes as a "thin mystery" based on the first U-boat sighting on the East Coast by a lobster fisherman in 1941 in Penobscot Bay.

Luke

Anne Whitney Pierce

L uke was born on a stormy January day, a day when the rest of
Coombs Island did the usual winter things — baked or chopped
wood or mended lobster traps or painted buoys. His mother Emma
woke to a smokey sky and the first labor pains at around six o'clock in
the morning. None of the boys was stirring yet, and her husband Roy
was still sleeping, which was rare, even for a winter morning when he
didn't have to haul.

Emma slipped quietly out of the bedroom with a bundle of clothes,
clothes she'd worn for weeks on end and would burn after the baby
was born, and got dressed by the wood stove, looking out over the
still harbor. She stoked the fire and went outside. The cold air woke
her where the first pains had only roused her. Emma shivered with
the heat of her bulk and her mounting pain, looked up at the sky. The
air was thick wet with the promise of a storm.

Emma had trouble fitting her huge belly under the steering wheel
of the truck, but she managed by sitting just to one side. The key
broke through a thin crust of ice and turned over like a charm. The
Cross Road was slick with morning frost, but Emma drove fast,
knowing every bump and curve along the way and how the truck

hugged them. In six minutes she had gotten herself over to the Medical Center on the other side of the island.

Back at home Roy woke up and found Emma gone. He got some rope and lugged Emma's armchair outside, hoisting it onto the roof of the Dodge and tying it on as best he could. The sun had started to rise, what little of it was showing its face, and the roads were dry. On the ride over, Roy turned on the radio and lit a cigarette, went to work at waking up. He hadn't meant to oversleep that day.

"Just one of those things that happens when it's not supposed to," he told Emma when he got over to the hospital.

"More likely because it wasn't supposed to," Emma said. "I told you today was the day."

Everyone on Coombs Island knew that Emma Carter's babies were punctual, and the hospital was expecting her. The best room, the one with a bed covered with Sadie Rice's prize-winning quilt and a view of the harbor, had been made ready — the sheets turned down. It was the bed she had always lain in to give birth and never for too long.

Emma bumped into Colby Eaton at the check-in desk, his hand all wrapped up in an old rag and blood showing through. Seems Colby had sliced up his hand that morning on the inboard of his skiff when he reached down to grab his sinking bait knife. Colby clutched his knife in his good hand and Emma held a watch she'd brought to time the contractions.

"Seventy-six years old, Colby," Emma said. "Ain't you done with fishing yet?"

"Not likely," he said. "And how 'bout you, Emma? Six sons not enough?"

Emma chuckled. "You take the good bed, Colby," she said, "you may be here a while."

"Don't make no difference to me," Colby said, "I'd just as soon look at the road."

"You go ahead, Colby," Emma said again. "I won't be needing the harbor room this time. I'll be in and out in a half bit."

But it was to be a long labor with Luke, longer than any of her other six, stretching on through the raw day and into the night. And when they sent old Colby home later that day, Emma did move into the harbor room. At dusk, Bambi Fess, the night nurse and the girlfriend of Emma's oldest boy, came on duty.

"You must be getting old, Emma," she said. "I expected you to be long gone by the time I got here."

"Age has got nothing to do with it," Emma snapped. "It's just that this one's already got some beef with this crazy world. He don't want to come out just yet, and I can't say as I blame him."

When the pain wasn't so bad, Emma stood at the window looking out at the shadows of the sleeping boats and the churning water. When the tightening began in her belly, she would sit in the armchair and breathe through the contraction, watching the stopwatch all the while. Roy stayed outside in the waiting room, as he had done while all of his boys were coming into the world, drinking coffee and smoking cigarettes, talking to all the island people that came and went, Edna Pearl with her puffy legs and young Dennis Alcore with a split lip. From time to time, Roy poked his head into the harbor room to see how Emma was doing, but she just shooed him away.

Emma sat in the armchair and tried to think some about this child she was about to bear, the one that came so slowly and with such reluctance. It would be another boy, of course — and blond like the rest. No one in Emma's family had girls, except her cousin Darlene, who had nothing but. That was what she and Roy made best together — sons — but this one would be the last. Emma planned to give up the whole shooting match after Luke. She had told the doctor to tie her tubes up tight, no mistake, while he was down there fiddling around, once and for all.

By dinnertime, Emma started getting restless, thinking of all the chores that needed doing around the house — ironing, scrubbing, mending — impatient that she wasn't home to do them yet, a stranger to empty time. She wasn't much given to sitting still and thinking, and there wasn't much thinking left to do, anyway not about the baby's name. Early on she'd decided to call him Luke, and no one in the family had thought to change her mind. None of the other boys had been named until a week or so after he was born. That was the rule Emma made after Frank, her first son, whom she'd planned to name Dean after Dean Martin. But Dean just never stuck, and she had to change his name from Dean Frank to Frank Dean.

"You can't possibly name a baby till you've been acquainted some good long while," Emma claimed. "Look at Frankie Dean."

People did look at Frankie Dean. Like all of Emma's sons, he was a good-looking boy, fair, with soft skin and a strong build.

But this one had been Luke from the start. It was Emma's father's name, and it had taken her this long, forty years and seven sons, and the old man's death, for her to blur the sour memories of her father's drinking and meanness, forty years and seven sons before she could give the name to one of her boys. It was fitting, for the last one to be Luke, and she was glad.

By ten o'clock the pains were coming closer. Dr. Bellin came into the room to examine Emma. He poked and probed and frowned. It was only the seventh baby he had ever delivered, and the first on Coombs Island.

"Why's your face all screwed up like scorched silk?" Emma asked him.

"You're still only five centimeters dilated, Mrs. Carter, and I'm afraid the baby's not in the proper position. Sunny-side up and turned to one side, if my hands don't lie. The labor's progressing too slowly, and when the baby does come, there may be trouble."

"We've been near to intimate," she said. "Call me Emma and tell me what you mean."

"I'd like to send you up to the hospital in Blue Hill, in case we have to do a Caesarean section," Dr. Bellin said.

Well, Emma let him have it then. Dr. Bellin, who was young and new to Coombs Island, didn't know that Emma wouldn't let any doctor, young or old, slice her open with a knife. Ten years back they'd said that lump on her neck might kill her, but she'd just let it be.

"All my children come naturally," Emma said crossly, "or they aren't entirely welcome. We'll just wait."

So they all waited for Luke to turn himself around — Emma and Roy and young Dr. Bellin and Bambi Fess, the other night nurse and two of the older Carter boys, who came by to see if they had another brother yet. Emma walked in circles, rubbing her stomach and coaxing Luke along. The pains started to come right on top of each other, but the baby was still twisted and wouldn't slide down. Dr. Bellin tried to give Emma pills to slow down the contractions, to give Luke more time to straighten himself out. But Emma pushed them away.

"He'll come when he's ready," she insisted, sweat dripping from her forehead onto her temples and the white sheet. "And how he gets here is his own business."

Lying there on the bed, exhausted and sore, Emma thought she saw the moon out the window, though she couldn't have, because the sky was still thick with storm clouds. As she shifted to get a better look at the sky, she felt a great surge in her belly. And in one long, thrashing motion, Luke Perry Carter turned himself around and announced himself properly to the world — dark crown first and without a sound.

Emma was weak and sore after the birth, hurting more than she could ever remember hurting, and that made her mad. But there was something rolled around in her mind that night, something about having just turned forty and feeling tired, something about having seven sons and being at peace with her father and done with child-birth, that softened her just a bit. She looked out the window where she saw only black rumbling skies and one escaped star from the dark Milky Way. She longed to hear the sound of the water lapping the sides of the sleeping winter boats, feel the salt mist spray her face, watch the gulls soar and dive. She closed her eyes to sense the things she missed lying there in that hospital bed.

"You still planning on going home right away, Emma?" Dr. Bellin asked. He'd heard that all of Emma's babies spent their first night at home, that neither Roy nor any of the boys had ever missed one of Emma's home-cooked meals for something as simple as having a baby.

"I think I'll rest here awhile," Emma said, her eyes closing slowly. "Luke and I'll be up early, home in time to make breakfast and pack the boys off to school." Her voice drifted off, and Bambi Fess took Luke to get cleaned up.

"Don't bring him back till morning, Bambi," Emma told her drows-ily. "My milk's not in yet, and he won't be needing me till then. I'll get some rest, and then we'll meet properly."

Luke was the only baby in the nursery that night. In fact, there had never been more than one baby at a time in the Coombs Island Medical Center nursery except when Emma had the twins six years before. January was a slow time for babies, Emma told Bambi that night, because most babies got started in winter, not born, when folks were cold and had lots of time on their hands. She didn't know what she and Roy had been thinking of, starting Luke in the spring like they had. "Just a couple of April fools, I guess," she said.

Bambi and the other night nurse whispered about Luke, the long, dark baby that never made a peep. He wasn't the kind of baby you wanted to cuddle or pet, or tie ribbon in his hair, though Luke had plenty of soft black fuzz. He didn't seem to need anything, lay pa-tiently while Bambi wiped off the blood and the white film that covered him.

"This baby knows something," Bambi told the other night nurse. "What?" she asked. "Something," she said. "Something most people will never know," she said.

After Bambi wrapped him in a blanket and laid him down, the girls just let him be. It was too bad, Bambi thought, because he was probably the only baby they'd see for a while, the whole of winter being a slow time for babies and her friend Ramona not due till March.

And so while Emma slept a deep, dreamless sleep, Luke spent his first night alone, watchful and not unhappy in his tiny bed. Emma woke at dawn her old self, burly and strong and running every show. She ordered ham and eggs for breakfast and when she found out the kitchen hadn't opened yet, she went down and made it herself.

"Where's my son?" she asked the day nurse, whose name she didn't know. Luke came to her wide-eyed, and she offered him a full breast, which he took to without instruction or comment. When he was done on one side, she took him over by the window and raised him up high in the light. The storm had blown out to sea. The sun sparkled on the harbor boats; the gulls swooped and squawked with news of an early spring. Turning the baby around, Emma studied him at different angles, staring into the dark eyes, waiting for him to blink.

"You're some different than the other boys, aren't you, Luke?" she asked.

Luke hiccupped back at her and Emma set him at her other breast. And as he suckled, with wide, unblinking eyes, Luke told her that he was.

Anne Whitney Pierce lives in Cambridge, Massachusetts, where she awaits the birth of her second child. Her work has been published in *The Boston Globe Magazine, The Virginia Quarterly Review*, and *New Age Journal*.

Whose Maine Island?
Caliban's or Ariel's?

Constance Hunting

When I first fetched up on these wilder shores — that is, crossed, in the watershed year, 1968, the bridge at Kittery —I felt that I had entered a different country rather than simply crossed a state border. I felt, in fact, that I had arrived on an island. And, in a sense, I was right. "Maine" *is* an island, a separate territory, metaphorically as well as geographically. I felt like Ferdinand.

Ferdinand, you may recall, fetches up, along with others of the Naples court crowd, on Prospero's island in Shakespeare's "The Tempest."

I have a friend, born and brought up in Blue Hill, Maine, who claims that people who live on islands are different from those who live on the mainland. Islanders are connected to the mass of their fellow human beings by the most tenuous fibers — a wake in the water, a suspension bridge. They are independent; they may also become ingrown. Perspectives, my friend suggests, get skewed. What elsewhere is perceived as commendable may here be seen as undesirable. *Much* becomes little; and *little* becomes much. And Maine, perhaps even more strongly than the rest of New England, retains its

Puritan heritage. The very fierceness against which this heritage may be fought underscores its continuing force. Mix the Puritan suspicion of the arts and the maxims handed down to children — "You can't put a sunset on the table," "Don't expect any hand-outs," "Who do you think you are?" (good question) — with little but weather to learn higher truths from, and you have a situation that, you might think, would make an Ariel weep.

Ariel was Prospero's sprite-slave in "The Tempest," creature of air, fire, water, opposite to his other slave, the earth-bound Caliban, the "monster," the "thing most brutish," carrier of logs and catcher of fish. A signal difference between Ariel and Caliban, aside from their obvious physical properties, is that Ariel can *get away* from the island. If you can "ride/On the curl'd clouds" at least once in a while, you're going to have a less intense relationship to it.

But Caliban can't get away. He is island-bound. He doesn't see, hear, touch, or smell anything but the island he was born on. It is true that when Prospero arrives, exiled from Milan, Caliban trusts him; but he later feels that Prospero has taken his island from him by virtue of intellect, learning, breadth of experience, and knowledge. Caliban is not stupid; rather, his intelligence is simply in a state of nature. He regards what we might call Prospero's "virtues" as manifestations of superior guile. And because he's such a plain-living monster, when the storm brewed by Prospero and engineered by Ariel washes up Ferdinand along with the silly, meritricious court hangers-on Trinculo, Stephano, et cetera, Caliban is dazzled by these drunken schemers, thinks them "gods," "wondrous men." He has nothing to compare them to. They're the first tourists he's seen. He has the gullibility of the innocent, the isolated. The allegiance which Prospero has dashed, Caliban instantly transfers to Trinculo.

High-flying Ariel shows no such change of loyalty. To him, Prospero remains ever "my potent master." Indeed, the two slaves exchange only a few words in five acts. When Caliban tells Trinculo that Prospero is a "tyrant" and a "sorcerer" who has cheated him of his island, Ariel says, "Thou liest." Caliban retorts, "I would my noble master [Trinculo] would destroy thee." It is as though they occupy different sides of the island.

Have we strayed far from Maine? Not really. For Maine, that metaphorical and geographical "island," possesses, and perhaps more clearly than other territories, its antithetical "sides," as shown best, for our purposes, in its literature. Maine has produced two distinct strains of writing: the genteel and the "new" realistic. Examples of the former would include the novels of, say, Mary Ellen Chase, Gladys Hasty Carroll, and Elizabeth Coatsworth; of the latter, the work of Carolyn Chute, Sanford Phippen, and John Gould (of *The Greenleaf Fires*). The two strains differ in subject matter, tone, style, and diction, as well as in structural and metaphysical standards.

The primary definition of "genteel" includes such qualities as elegance, gracefulness, refinement, and freedom from vulgarity or rudeness; the secondary definition includes such faintly negative modifications as "striving to maintain the appearance of superior or middle-class social status or respectablity" (we've dropped back a rung on the ladder), "marked by false delicacy, prudery, or affectation," "conventionally or insipidly pretty." All of these secondary characteristics of "genteel" are not only antipathetic, they are anathema to art. Our serious "genteel" novelists need not fear them. Here, however, is an example of the qualities of the secondary definition, the opening of a collection of stories, as it happens, published in 1953; but oh, it has served in many a Maine novel of similar ilk (a genteel word):

> On a glorious morning in June, in the year 1905, I sat resting on a wayside boulder atop a high ridge overlooking a verdant valley through the middle of which the Aroostook River wended its leisurely way along intermittent stretches of clearing and primeval forest. . . .
> (*Maine Stories*, by John William Stolle)

Precisely this sort of writing is satirized by Sanford Phippen in the opening of "Cocktails on the Point," in his 1982 collection *The Police Know Everything*:

> It had been a perfect August day on the coast of Maine, one of those few late summer days with no fog or even any haze. The waters of French-man Bay sparkled brilliantly in the sunlight, the leaves of the deciduous trees stirred ever so sensuously in the slight warm breeze. Many summer folk had gone a-sailing. . . .

The difference is one of intent as well as of talent. The first writer's style is received: this is how you do it. You take pen in hand. Your handwriting is consciously ornate, "pretty" — sitting on a big rock by the side of the road is not like "resting on a wayside boulder." Since the month is June, the reader would be surprised if the grass were *not* green. So perhaps "verdant" could be left to implication. If a river wends, it generally does so in leisurely fashion; one does not often see a roaring river wending. Phippen has chosen a perfect style to parody for a purpose: not the style itself but the affectedness of the social level that encourages it. If the August day is perfect, sunlight is implied. Frenchman Bay implies water, and leaves imply deciduous trees.

Contrast these openings with that of the title story of Phippen's collection: "Whenever I'm down home on the coast visiting with my mother on the weekends, I usually try to stop by and have a chat with my Aunt Bunny Crowley, Taunton Ferry's oldest living policman." Or this, from Ruth Moore's novel *A Fair Wind Home* (1953): "The Lord only knew what Edward Ellis had been up to or where he had been for three years, but he had certainly brought home some finc presents."

We immediately sense that these authors' voices are close to the characters they are going to tell us of; we immediately sense the social level of the characters through the level of language employed. Further, we apprehend that since Phippen's narrator "usually" — not "always" — visits with Aunt Bunny on his weekends "down home," Taunton Ferry has other residents whom we are going to come to know. We sense that we're going to find out not only what presents Edwara Ellis has brought to his family but where he has been and what he has been doing for those three mysteriou. years. These openings are neither received nor imported; they are, so to say, custom-made on the spot.

Openings are where the writer casts the spell. Let us consider two more:

> Mary Peters first saw Cadiz in 1880. She was nine years old then. She had awakened early to the swift knowledge that the ship was quiet, not plunging or rolling, not pitching or swooping, not whining or groaning in her bolts and beams or rattling her gear, not even perceptibly swinging to the tide, but instead, still, tranquil, idle.

We note first the prose, the balance and simplicity and exactitude of the language — which is probably not that of Mary Peters, the protagonist of Mary Ellen Chase's 1934 novel of that name. We thus apprehend that the narrator is at a greater remove from the narrative than in the Phippen and Moore offerings. A nine-year-old would not be likely to think in just those words, although she could comprehend what was happening in just that way. And, as the narrator is at a greater distance, so the events in this opening carry with them long shadows of which we are not immediately aware. Not until later do we understand the significance of Cadiz in Mary Peters' metaphorical life, nor that "the ship" is indeed at a standstill — that the industry which it represents is dying in New England ports. Symbolism has entered this literary level.

The Junkyard: Sunday, 7 a.m.

The scout crow, lean in winter, makes a sweep over the outer ring of wrecks and junks. Everything is sealed in new snow. The scout crow opens his toes and swings down to perch on the boom of the yard tractor. He checks for signs of life but finds only the now-and-then plop of snow from hoods and fenders.

Over the Drugstore: Same time.

The room is hot and the bedcovers are in a ball on the floor. The only thing Crowe Bovey is wearing is his metal-rimmed glasses. He pokes at Jill Luce. . . .

Different again! The opening of Carolyn Chute's "Crowe Bovey's Burning-Cold," from her novel-in-progress, casts its spell chiefly through symbolic force at once evident to the reader. Crow. Crowe. One crow, sorrow. Cold. Lifelessness. Heat. Light of a sort: Luce. Jill-chill? "C/hecks" and "pokes" are slant-rhymes, connecting each section to the other. And so on. All of these responses happen with extreme rapidity in the reader's mind and pass into his reading subconscious. We do not know, on the factual level, what precipitates the story, but we sense opposing factors strongly at work, and a stark urgency in the narrator's eerily disembodied voice. Furthermore, there is a seeming split or conflict between the non-human level of the first section and the social level hinted at in the second. And the use of the present tense has the effect of making time timeless — "Same time." Clearly, the mind behind this opening is possessed of an extraordinary imagination, an imagination which refuses labels, if it even notices them. If, as Marguerite Yourcenar maintains, writers do not create, but arrange, this arranger is amazingly close to creating.

Characters reveal writers as surely as writers reveal characters.

What these arbitrarily selected writers — save the first — have in common is lack of condescension towards their characters. Condescension is likely to lead to patronization of language and hence to patronization of the reader, who, if he is the kind of reader writers want, will resent it. The writers exemplified here, whether their visions are comic, tragic, or something between, give characters their due as human beings. But to what sort of characters do they choose, or are they able, to give their due? Which side of the island do they explore, Caliban's or Ariel's?

In falsely genteel Maine literature, which of course does not know it is false, emphasis and point of view focus on upper, or what passes for upper, and middle class characters. The captain, the lawyer, the doctor, the teacher, the bountiful housewife, the rosy children (*one* of whom may, however, be sickly, perhaps die). The lower classes appear, if at all, as foils or as vaudeville relief — the Canuck who talks funny, by Gar, dat; the tippling stagecoach driver; the poacher who traps himself. Nothing new in this, we may say; Shakespeare did it. But then we recall that to Shakespeare, Audrey and Bottom and Verges, and even Caliban, were as fully human (and interesting) as any Wolsey, Bassanio, Cloten, or Prospero. In the literature that we are discussing, the lower orders, as society dictates, are used as fictional levers to increase the elevation of the middle and upper classes, of which every village has its representatives. The difference between the Bimmet tribe in *Maine Stories* and the Greels in *The Police Know Everything* is the difference in attitude of the writers towards their characters. The "bewhiskered farmer of some seventy summers" — there's false gentility for you! — who introduces the narrator-from-away in the black derby hat to the County, classified the Bimmets as "all alike — a dirty streak in every ghostly one of 'em. Put 'em all in a big sack together and shake 'em up, and 'twouldn't make a mite of difference which one would come out first — he'd bear watchin'." Enter Bimmets, Bimmets dismissed, with the informant's, the narrator's, the author's, and hence the reader's superior chuckle.

The Greels, too, are a tribe. But Phippen integrates them with other characters of Taunton Ferry, including Aunt Bunny's cat, Henry:

"Henry has a mind of his own, don't ya, Henry? He's just as sneaky as that awful Calvin Hayes and the Greels."
"What do you mean?"

"Well, we police spend most of our time trying to track 'em down. They're always up to something. The other night Inez and I were on patrol down on the Point when we come upon Calvin and the Greels... he's always up to no good, running with those awful Greels. . . . They said they were just cutting blowdowns, but I knew better. Cripes! They were cutting trees off other people's land and selling the wood. And that Calvin Hayes, struttin' around just like a little cock bantam."

"Isn't he the blonde boy in the red sports car who flooded the tennis courts last summer?"

The red sports car would seem to indicate a different social level from that of the Greels, which is different from that of policewoman Bunny, which is different from that of the narrator who, born and raised in Taunton Ferry, has gone away to university and now teaches at the high school in a university town. Yet here they are, individuals mingled and connected by the fact that Phippen sees them, whatever their stations, as human beings. In his preface to *The Police Know Everything*, Phippen states, "like people in real life, my characters are simply representatives of both the funny and the tragic, existing always together at the same time, and sometimes crossing over." Phippen thus cannot be tempted by the "quaintness" which lesser writers of Maine allow. The smiles he draws from readers do not result from a dismissal of, but a recognition of, the inexhaustible variety and ingenuity of human nature.

In his 1980 article, "Missing from the Books: My Maine," Phippen asks, "So what is it that Maine writers, especially ones from away, need to know about Maine natives that will help them avoid this constant and patronizing stereotyping and shallow characterization?" And answers: "[They] need to know more about the poverty and frustration, the thwarted ambition and lack of opportunity, the bitterness and uneasiness that goes back many generations and underlies everything." Once they know, they can understand, he suggests; the artistic lens will then widen and they can begin to write truly, with all their diverse talents. Caliban's side of the island, as well as Ariel's, must be explored. Talent, temperament, and literary and existential influences will play a part in each writer's response.

How well Mary Ellen Chase knows her side of the island! In *Mary Peters* she writes of a Maine (her Maine) which is half-unaware that it is caught in the middle of the old and the new, between the great seafaring days when "foreign ports were household words" and "doorstones of solid slabs of Maine coast granite were set about with rare Pacific shells," and the days of rusticators and entrepreneurs who would change not only the social fabric of Petersport but also its citizen's patterns within it. It is more the case of not being able to know the village until you have known the world than the reverse; it is less the world than worldliness that is shrinking the village's possibilities. Chase delineates the social levels of Petersport through to "certain outskirts of the town where lived the less substantial of its people — labourers of sorts, fishermen, those who had once worked at its docks. . . . Their women did the washing and spring cleaning of larger houses. . . ." Chase shows the reader her own view of the village through the eyes of Mary Peters' mother, who has sailed with her captain husband the seas of the world:

> Sarah Peters knew the village character better through sailing away from it for many years than if she had lived close at hand with it. She, like others of her heritage and nurture, had a perspective upon it that it could never have upon itself. She recognized that shrewdness native to the New England rural mind, a shrewdness steadily developed through two centuries and more by struggle with land and sea, by the necessity for thrift and quick thinking and the seizing of opportunity. She knew that . . . under the mellowing influences of contact with other lands and other minds, that shrewdness lost itself in a humourous kind of wisdom; she knew, too, that under more narrowing influences it doubled back upon itself, becoming more acute, more subtle, cunning even.

So far, so good. And her recognition of the native mind's "shrewdness" in quickly seizing "opportunity" reminds of Aunt Bunny Crowley's assessment of the Greels: "The Greels steal what they need. You can't get ahead of 'em. There'll always be Greels, for they're good breeders."

But the Greels do not appear in the purlieu of Sarah Peters. Mary Ellen Chase never goes further along that road from the village, further back, further in; never, in this novel, crosses to Caliban's side of the island. Perhaps she could not. Some of those who have glimpsed it cannot bring themselves to treat of it. They are repelled by its mire, and thus denied the radiance of Yeats' understanding of where "love has pitched his tent." They forget that in Shakespeare's play it is Ariel who leads Trinculo, Stephano, and Caliban "through/Tooth'd briers, sharp furzes, prickling goss, and thorns" till they fall into "the filthy mantled pool. . . . There dancing up to the chins, that the foul lake/O'erstunk their feet." Although Trinculo wails, "Monster, I do smell all horse piss," Caliban has scarcely noticed the misadventure; and we note that the pool is "just beyond" Propsero's "cell." We note also that Prospero's response to Ariel is, "That was well done, my bird."

Among current Maine writers, it is Carolyn Chute who comes closest to exploring the whole island. But, some will protest, she writes only of the Calibans. The tribe of Greels; the Beans. She's turned over the "boulder" we were resting on, that glorious morning in June. The vermin rush out. She's spilled the beans.

But Chute's view is — aerial, an aerial of the earth. She is the crow who sweeps and swoops and checks for "signs of life." Just now, and high time, the signs of life on this island are on Caliban's side.

In the final scene of "The Tempest," Prospero *frees* Ariel; he *pardons* Caliban. He thus allows the monster his portion of humanity. In his gratitude, Caliban promises — and we believe him — to "be wise hereafter,/And seek for grace." Remarkable word in a monster's mouth! He realizes he has been "a thrice double ass . . . to take this drunkard [Trinculo] for a god/And worship this dull fool!" Pardoned, his real nature can assert itself, balance bogs and brine-pits with fresh springs and sweet airs, name the lights, the lesser and the greater. . . . Well, perhaps. He has been given that chance, at any rate, by Prospero, who in one of his guises is art.

Before the curtain falls — or rises? — let us recall those "strange shapes" that greet Shakespeare's shipwrecked banqueters, one of whom says:

If in Naples
I should report this now, would they believe me?
If I should say I saw such islanders
(For certes, these are people of the island,)
Who, though they are of monstrous shape, yet, note,
Their manners are more gentle, kind, than of
Our human generation you shall find
Many, any, almost any.

Whose island? Can we choose?

Constance Hunting is a lecturer in Creative Writing and Literature at the University of Maine in Orono. She is the author of five books of poetry and is the publisher and editor of Puckerbrush Press Books and *Puckerbrush Review*.